"A bouquet of diverse stories, *We've Been There* illustrates the uniqueness and complexity found in every adoptee's journey. The importance and courage of sharing your story is evident on every page and will inspire everyone to have more nuanced and meaningful conversations around adoption."

—KATI POHLER, 25, China, featured on BBC Stories'
Meet Me on the Bridge

"In *We've Been There*, adoptive mother Susan TeBos shares insights gleaned from the many teenaged and young adult adoptees whom she has interviewed. Some disclose the trauma they suffered as young children, some delve into what abandonment feels like, and all are candid about the particular ways their adoptions continue to affect their senses of self and their mental health. By collecting and sharing their stories, TeBos offers comfort and hope to teenaged adoptees."

—JENNIFER GRANT, author of *Dimming the Day* and *Love You More*

"Easy to read and filled with affirming aha moments, *We've Been There* demonstrates that when our stories connect, we find a little bit more community and a little bit more hope that we'll be okay."

—COREY METTLER, MA, LPC, Adoption Therapist,
Families Forever Counseling

"Stacks of books have been written for adoptive parents, but few have been published with a teen-adoptee audience in mind. In this book, Susan TeBos brings a sweet gift to the hands of adoptees—a book uniquely tailored for them, relating to their joys, pains, sorrows, and achievements. Through these stories, Susan and her adoptee contributors walk the reader through a journey of confidence, loneliness, trust, answered (and unanswered) questions, and acceptance. In these pages, you'll find a kindred spirit that will encourage, strengthen, and equip you to confidently embrace the story God has written for your life."

—LEAH JOLLY, 21, domestic adoptee

"As a family support network with more than 25 years of experience, Families for Russian & Ukrainian Adoption (FRUA) knows adoption is a lifelong journey. We find children go through phases of connection to their adoption, an ebb and flow of emotions toward their birth parents, birth culture, and heritage. Susan TeBos's book validates the feelings and resiliency many of our FRUA Young Adult Club members have expressed."

—MJ KAMEN, chair of Families for Russian & Ukrainian Adoption, www.frua.org

"A wonderfully insightful and refreshing read for anyone who's experienced adoption. Susan TeBos cleverly combines the God-and-grit ingredients found in every adoption story, and the result is like *Chicken Soup for the Adopted Soul*. I plan to give this book to my own teenagers, and expect they will be intrigued to find themselves comparing their own circumstances and feelings surrounding adoption to those they read about in this book."

—JIM SPRAGUE, adoptive father

"Thank you, teens, for the peek inside your hearts and minds, for sharing your feelings and thoughts. Your stories have helped me come to a greater understanding. I have new ideas on how I can ask questions, listen, and pray."

—ROBERTTA DEVRIES, adoptive mother

"As a grateful adoptive mom of six, I am confident this book will not only abundantly bless adoptees, but also all those who are party to adoption. It is full of practical advice and contains numerous glimpses of love amidst the many relationships that surround adoption. Though heart-wrenching struggles pepper many of these stories, hope shines through."

—BETH SCHNYDERS, adoptive mother

WE'VE BEEN THERE

True **STORIES,** *Surprising* **INSIGHTS,**
and Aha **MOMENTS** *for* **ADOPTED TEENS**

Susan TeBos

KREGEL
PUBLICATIONS

TO THE STORYTELLERS IN
THIS BOOK WHOSE HONESTY
AND VOICE IS A GIFT TO ALL
WHO OPEN THESE PAGES

CONTENTS

ON OPENING UP

When you have the courage to look squarely at your losses, and to grieve them, you're finally free to fully embrace the life you have today. As you do, know that you are not alone. The One who loves you is with you, as is the great siblinghood of other adoptees—who you may not even know—who share your journey. You can do this.

MARGOT STARBUCK
Adoptee, adoptive mom, and author

IF YOU'RE READING this book, I know a little something about you. You're curious—curious about what others who were adopted are thinking and feeling and experiencing. In a way, you crave a little intel into their lives because you're hoping to make sense of things going on in your own life. And why not? It's only natural to want to connect with other young people who share a common bond. If anything, it will help just to hear what they have to say—and bonus, you'll never wonder if you are alone in this again.

My daughter, a recent high school graduate, had this to say: "I did feel pretty alone in my thoughts about my separation story, simply because other adopted people in my life never shared deep things. I like being able to see what other people struggle with. We all handle it in different ways. I want to see how other people have dealt with it and what has come of it."

Sound like something you're thinking? Welcome aboard. We'll cover a lot of ground in these pages: sometimes hard, often good, but always hopeful. Among the short stories . . .

A cheerleader opens up about feeling defective.

A film student explains how he handles social anxiety.

A college finance major learns how to manage his emotions before he explodes.

A junior in high school grieves the loss of her birth father, whom she never met.

From finding oneself on a study abroad in Shanghai, to wrestling with God about fitting in or not belonging, or just living with too much self-doubt, every person I talked with was open about feelings and situations they had rarely, if ever, spoken about before. I am proud of them for stepping up, looking back, sharing their intimate thoughts and experiences, and when possible, making sense of what was going on—all for you. I appreciate them for showing you it is okay to open up to a trusted ally, and the sooner the better. They would say we need stories. We need each other. We need to be real and tell it like it is. These are their stories—no fake smiles, no perfect selfies.

ABOUT THE PEOPLE YOU'LL MEET

This book began with an invitation I posted on social media that fanned out across the nation. It went something like this:

> If you're a young adult who was adopted and currently between the ages of sixteen and thirty, tell us about a time when you were a teen, good, bad, or otherwise.

Open up about how your separation story had impacted you—unfiltered, of course. In other words, give us an honest glimpse of your journey including how you made it through the tough times, if any, plus any advice or insight you have to share.

One by one, adopted teens and young adults ages fifteen to thirtysomething responded to me from Florida, Louisiana, Texas, Minnesota, the Great Lakes, Pittsburgh, New Jersey, and down the East Coast. A handful contacted me from universities in Michigan, and a few others from local high schools in my hometown. Many took their first breath in Russia, China, Vietnam, Ethiopia, Kenya, Guatemala, and South Korea—and some right here in the US.

We met face-to-face when possible, or on Zoom, FaceTime, and email too. I asked questions, they opened up, and I was drawn in by their honest, sometimes flailing attempts to put words to their feelings of rejection, loss, depression, anxiety, or fear of being abandoned again and how these feelings affected them. I was equally touched by those who had questions and wondered and were working it out. You'll see a range of responses.

WHY READ THE SHORT STORIES IN THIS BOOK?

There's a simple and excellent reason for you to read the experiences of others who have been adopted: to help you sort things out. It's a first step worth considering. Perhaps you will relate to something someone says or to someone struggling with stuff similar to yours. Maybe you'll be inspired. Or you'll make a better decision because someone worked through something that gave you renewed hope. Wouldn't it be nice to know you are not the only one who feels the way you do? To hear what others have to say?

You can approach the stories in several ways. You do you.

- Read from start to finish. You might be surprised.
- Read randomly, kind of like surfing through TikTok. You never know what you'll find that will make you laugh or cry or inspire you.
- Read a section. Let the tug of your heart and curiosity pull you where you need to go.
- Let someone else read the book first and point out stories just for you, especially if reading isn't your thing.

Here's the thing. My guess is that you'll find yourself in a story or two. Let them speak to you. Then consider this: What if you don't outgrow your separation story but instead grow *into* it, in a healthy way? What if you have to look at it to see it? Talk about it to understand it? Say it out loud and reorganize it to accept it? And feel it firsthand to grieve it and release it? It's what many of the teens and young adults I interviewed did over time. Easy? No. First steps usually aren't. But they found that opening up and revealing the invisible things hidden in their hearts was the path forward and well worth it.

Think no one else knows what it's like? Think again. Inside these pages you may just find a kindred spirit who thinks and feels the way you do. Take a look.

DARE TO OVERCOME

WRESTLING IS A PART OF LIFE

Courage doesn't mean you don't get afraid.
Courage means you don't let fear stop you.

BETHANY HAMILTON

CHAPTER 1

BRAVE

You sort of start thinking anything's possible if you've got enough nerve.

J. K. ROWLING

MATTHEW WAS ADOPTED in 1998 from Surgut, a sprawling oil-drilling city in Siberia where temperatures can drop as low as -60 degrees Fahrenheit. At birth he barely tipped the scale at six pounds. His adoption documents say his birth mother was thirty-five when she gave birth to him in a hospital. Then she left.

Matt has one picture of himself as an infant wrapped in a hospital receiving blanket like a fresh loaf of Russian brown bread. For seven and a half months, he camped out in a crib, alone, losing out on what all babies need. Not a single visitor came until he was adopted by his American parents.

Today, Matt is twenty-one. He's a friendly, good-looking guy but considers himself awkwardly quiet when you first meet him. He's rocking a scruffy beard and wearing blue titanium glasses that make him look like a typical college guy, which he is. His black hair, tight curls, and warm olive skin make me think he's more Greek or Italian than Russian. I ask him what he knows about his birth ancestry, and he smirks and smiles. Recently he took an Ancestry DNA test. "My parents gave it to me for my birthday." Turns out he's half Russian and a delicious Mediterranean tossed salad mix of Greek, Turkish, and Italian. He says it was a great discovery. At least now he knows where his birth father came from, and who he looks like. Like others who dive into their DNA history, there's usually someone fascinating swimming in the gene pool. Turns out Matt is also related through DNA to Otzi the Iceman, a fully preserved European male from around 3300 BC discovered in a glacier between Austria and Italy. Fascinating! Now I get the smirk.

Matt is a college junior. He is studying film and sound. He's attracted to a wide range of music from EDM to Christian pop, loves every last *Fast and Furious* movie including the *Hobbs and Shaw* spin-off, and enjoys virtual reality games like *Beat Saber*. He holds down two part-time jobs, one on campus working in audiovisual for campus events and one down the road at another college as part of an audiovisual setup crew and event stager. All the while, he struggles with social anxiety.

"It hasn't been easy," Matt says when we sit down to talk. He tells me his social anxiety peaked in middle school and high school, not to the point that it derailed his life but enough that he had to deal with nervous habits and trouble talking to random people in the halls and between classes.

"I'd get sweaty hands," he says. He describes his anxiety as a domino effect: whatever is going on inside his head triggers his body to cue the sweaty palms and uncomfortable feelings . . . especially when dealing with people he doesn't know.

"I try to be nice, because I'm a nice guy, but it can get awkward."

Especially in high school, he was self-conscious and afraid of what people thought about him.

"It's just how my brain rolled. I have a mix of social anxiety and general anxiety, my own self-diagnosis. I call it an anxiety fusion. It's this piece about me that I don't like. It gets exhausting."

Even at twenty-one, he still battles social anxiety to some degree, sweaty palms included, although he says it's getting better as he gets older. So I ask him how he deals with his version of social anxiety. I'm sitting at the table while he paces, anticipating my questions.

"What happens when you're in film class?" I ask.

"I am a wallflower."

"What does that mean?"

"I stand in the back of the small group in the studio and watch. I pay attention, but I don't make any executive decisions." Pausing to think, he says he prefers to lead from behind the scenes. I say, "That's perfect. More people should do that." He smiles.

"What about the classroom?" I ask.

"If the subject matter is intriguing, I might join in on the conversation. If the professor points at me, in my head I say, *Crap!* But I answer."

"I get the impression you don't like to be seen, or maybe you're just shy. What about interviewing for a job, such as a summer job or internship? You have two."

"Interviewing stresses me out, but I still do it." He frowns. "There was one time when I had to talk to a guy at church about an audiovisual internship. Everything inside my head screamed, *Freeze!*"

Matt says he had to push himself and go against all instincts or miss out on a great opportunity.

"What about dating?" We lock eyes and he shakes his head.

"I imagine I can push through. Maybe five minutes into the date I say I have social anxiety."

"You're actually going to spit it out like that?" I laugh. "Bravo."

"Yeah! And I hope the other person says, 'I do too'."

"Wow! That's quite an icebreaker."

He admits, with a laugh, that dating is on hold or that maybe he and his best friend will remain single forever.

"What about friends? Does it seem harder to make friends when you have, as you call it, an anxiety fusion?"

"Making friends in high school is different for everyone. I mean, we all have some degree of anxiety then."

Matt met some of his best friends in a six-by-three-foot sound booth running sound and lighting for school events.

"When you're in that close proximity, it's a great place to make friends. It's easy when you're around a few familiar faces."

He says he felt uncomfortable when someone new stepped into the booth.

"I just had to step up and push through the uncomfortable feelings."

Being in the sound booth in high school got Matt interested in sound, lighting, and film. He says it was incredible, like a whole new world opened up for him.

"Ask me to step onto the stage in front of a crowd, and I go from awkward to disabled. Ask me to light the stage and unmute mics, and I suddenly become confident and capable. It's just how my brain rolls."

But that's not totally true. He mentions a brief one-time stint on stage during a dance-off battle between ten dorm sections.

"You were in a dance-off?" I question with a big smile on my face.

"Yeah," he laughs. "I liked working with our group of guys who choreographed our dance, but I knew them from the dorm. That's the difference."

Taking a huge risk, Matt joined his section team, and twenty guys learned to synchronize their hips to a Coldplay medley. Their section won third place.

"It was a lot of fun!" he says. "It was worth the risk."

Matt admitted to a lot of fear, failure, and self-doubt over the years. Recently, while creating a memoir piece for a class film project, he had what some might call an epiphany or turning point. He was watching a twenty-year-old VHS of his adoption while preparing for a film project for class.

"I saw myself as a baby in my dad's arms." Then he began filming the scene off the old VHS with a borrowed camera from the university.

"Suddenly, I wanted to tell myself something I don't tell myself enough."

That's when he began talking to the baby in the lens. "Be brave. Be oh-so-brave. You are going to do amazing things. Don't give up."

"Wow! You really said that?" I ask, a bit undone by his vulnerability.

"Yes. I just needed to tell this to my younger self."

"So were you making some sort of connection between anxiety and what you experienced as a baby?" He had spent the first critical months of his life alone.

"I think so. That makes sense," he says, with a thoughtful look on his face.

" I AM GETTING BRAVER EVERY DAY. IT'S SOMETHING YOU DON'T REALLY MASTER. YOU KEEP WORKING AT IT UNTIL YOU DIE.

"Are you brave?"

"I am getting braver every day. It's something you don't really master. You keep working at it until you die."

Then he begins to unpack some final pieces of wisdom for anyone like him.

"Be brave. Get those 'what-ifs' out of your head. Tell yourself not to get bogged down with negative thoughts, because there is a lot you will miss out on if you do—such as a chance to change your life, discover a career, have something big happen, make new friends, get a job, or even dance on stage someday. Don't let anxiety decide your next move. You decide. Sure, there are things we anxious types don't like and a million different things that go through our heads that can derail us. These imaginings rarely become reality. Like 99.9 percent of the time, these things don't happen. Trust me."

Matt wishes for a miracle cure for social anxiety.

"Maybe pushing ourselves, taking chances, and trusting ourselves more is the miracle."

Matt's social anxiety could have crippled him. But he found some things that helped: maturing, pushing through, learning it's okay and important to lead from behind the scenes, engaging in conversation even when it is uncomfortable, taking risks, practicing positive self-talk, and making healthy connections to his birth story.

CHAPTER 2

A TRUE FRIEND, MUSIC, AND GOD

We've all got both light and dark inside us.
What matters is the part we choose to act on.
That's who we really are.

J. K. ROWLING

PAUL WAS ADOPTED from South Korea when he was about two and a half years old and was raised in Oklahoma. As an infant he was found on the streets of Daegu. Today, he's a youth pastor in the Midwest. We met at his church on a Tuesday morning, sat at a table in the middle of the welcome center, and were constantly interrupted. That's because Paul is a people magnet. It's his gifting; he's just a really nice guy who loves to take care of others. So as people came and went, they chatted with him—even the UPS guy—and we talked in between.

I was interested in Paul's story because youth pastors have a certain way with teens; they're vulnerable and authentic and usually spill their guts on all things, including Jesus. Would an adopted youth pastor spill his story—like, seriously return to his teen years and confess? What Paul told me is only the tip of the iceberg when it comes to his life and the things God helped him overcome as a kid, teen, and adult, but he was willing to be honest.

"My two favorite activities as a teenager were running and music. Running helped me physically get my mind off a lot of the things that bothered me. When I ran, I could get away and leave my problems behind me."

Paul had found the "runner's high," a super healthy way to get outside of his head and leave the stress and negativity behind. As simple as it sounds, running made him feel satisfied with himself and life for a time. It was benefits like these that kept him lacing up his Nikes on a daily basis.

Paul says music helped him in a different way. "Sometimes I found myself at the piano for hours, just writing lyrics and composing music that fit how I felt about life, relationships, and God."

As an adopted child, Paul grew up wrestling with his identity and feelings of loneliness. He says shame haunted him so much that it led to anxiety, deep depression, and even suicidal thoughts. Music gave him an outlet to express his feelings and air his struggles.

"Most of my music was sad in words and in tone, but it was how I felt. Not all of my music was dark, though, as there were moments I expressed worship to God. Even though I struggled a lot as a teenager, I had hope in Christ."

Paul says his separation from his birth family and South Korea was a traumatic event that he believes affected him most as a teen.

"I have no knowledge of who my biological parents are or if I have any siblings. I don't even know my real birthday."

"How does that make you feel?" I ask.

"Back then it filled me with endless questions. Why would my parents just abandon me on the streets? How could they do this? Do my new parents really love me? Am I as valuable and precious to my new parents as their biological kids? Why do I keep having these nightmares that my adopted parents are going to stop somewhere and dump me off and then drive away? Why do kids at school make fun of my appearance? Why am I so ugly? Why can't I make friends?"

Throughout his teen years, questions hung over Paul. While running and music helped keep him going in life, it was relationships that mattered most. He says relationships have purpose and are the core of why we are alive.

"I am so thankful for my friend Scott. He was really my only friend throughout high school, but it only takes one good friend to make a huge difference. Scott was the type of guy you could share anything with, and he'd even cry with me. He was always there and never got mad at me for my emotional struggles. Instead, he'd even sing along with those depressing songs that I wrote."

"That's an amazing friend," I say.

"Music and friends have a way of helping us open up. Scott was the opposite of me in so many ways. He was popular, had many girlfriends in high school, was really handsome and outgoing, and he had many friends. Yet he mostly chose to spend his time with me because he truly cared about me. He was a gift from God in my life."

But the most important relationship that kept Paul going, he says, was with God.

"I can't tell you how many nights alone on my bed I would spend talking to God. Cry, laugh, and cry some more. I always knew in my heart that God was real and there was a reason I was adopted," he says.

Paul always thought being in America had a purpose. He just needed to be patient in the process. He says when a child has to go through the process of waiting for a family and being placed into a new home, there can be a lot of fears, worries, and uncertainties. And the longer the child has to wait, the worse the struggles can be.

"Yet God can turn any scary situation into something more beautiful than we can ever imagine if we put our trust in him." Paul quickly slips into youth pastor mode. It just comes out. He flips to Ephesians 1:5.

"It talks about how all of us, before time, were selected to be in God's family through Jesus. It doesn't matter our ethnicity, our background, or our talents. God is described as a Father who sees us as his children. God the Father wants to have a relationship with us."

"Why?" I ask.

"Because through a relationship with God we can find purpose for our lives."

"But you wrestled in your relationship with God as a teen," I press.

"I was fifteen. There was a time I didn't want to live, a time when I was at youth camp in the mountains of Colorado, and I left the group and found myself on the edge of a cliff. I thought I was going to die."

We sit at the table; he is gripping his Bible.

"Life is hard," he says. "God never promises that it will be easy."

He doesn't add any specifics. But I get the gist. That dark day on the mountain cliff changed him. His life was spared, and he was transformed. He told me that after high school he attended college and landed a camp ministry gig for a while that ultimately led him to his current position leading a church full of teens. He has finally found where he belongs.

> **YOU WILL KNOW YOU ARE HEALING WHEN YOU ARE LESS CONSUMED WITH YOURSELF AND MORE AWARE OF OTHERS.**

"I would encourage everyone who is reading this to seek God and to be prayerful and patient. The world is unfair sometimes. You can become bitter, feel like a victim, or fall into depression, but I encourage you to spend time with Jesus and find out that you are alive to be a blessing to people. You will know you are healing when you are less consumed with yourself and more aware of others. Find great friends, have an outlet, and come close to God. You will discover your purpose and identity as you grow in your relationship with God. It is all connected."

Paul struggled with feeling unworthy. His lack of self-worth undermined his day-to-day. If that sounds familiar, you might try some of the things that helped Paul: composing and writing music (or doing something creative that you enjoy, even if that's meticulously piecing together a thousand-piece Lego Titanic), running, hiking, biking, opening up to a good and loyal friend, or coming undone and releasing your anguish to God. In other words, if you don't like how you're feeling, do something that can make a difference. It worked for Paul. It can work for you.

CHAPTER 3

STANDING STRONG IN WHO YOU ARE

I always get to where I'm going by walking away from where I have been.

ALEX ROSS PERRY

I CONTACTED DIBORA, a high school senior who was adopted from Ethiopia when she was six. Over a period of two months, we got acquainted over the phone and hit it off right away. Dibora is eighteen. She loves Electric Cheetah's mouthwatering brisket sandwich, which she claims she cannot begin to explain the depths of how good it really is. It's that good. Since I knew the restaurant on her side of town that she raved about, I made a note to check out the brisket.

Dibora told me she's a regular latte girl—one shot of espresso with almond or soy milk, steamed. She wears rompers in the summer and jumpsuits in the fall. Heels are her favorite go-to footwear, but she was quick to add she can go from super fashionable to sweatpants and sneakers in a heartbeat. As a self-described extrovert and people lover, Dibora plans to study hospitality and tourism in college. God, family, and friends excite and energize her. And when she's not binge-watching

TikToks, hiking, or singing with earbuds in (she's been told she sings really bad), she's nestled on the couch with her older sister watching romantic comedies such as *Valentine's Day* or *To All the Boys I've Loved Before* (the first one; she says the sequel is too predictable).

What rocks Dibora's world?

When people don't stand up for themselves.

"I'm not afraid to stand up for myself," she says.

"So you're self-assured?" I clarify.

"Yeah. I like that. I am self-assured. I believe in myself."

Dibora radiates maturity beyond her years. She's earned her stripes the hard way. She's no stranger to trauma. As a child in Ethiopia, her first family was broken apart by disease and poverty. She says her parents carried her and her younger brother to an orphanage in Addis Abba and left them there rather than leave them to fend for themselves on the streets. They had no other choice.

Now an American teen and daughter of a white family, Dibora carries an unwanted burden: she's been bullied by classmates for being African, adopted, and having a white family.

"Sometimes when people see my family, they see that we're different. Yes, I have my birth family who gave me life. And yes, I have my parents who give me every chance in the world to have such a fantastic life."

But not everyone gets that. Especially a group of girls who made Dibora's sophomore year miserable by calling her "Oreo," a derogatory word for being black on the outside and white on the inside.

"The year I turned fifteen was the worst year ever. I was a sophomore, and I had to transfer schools when I didn't want to. I had to leave behind all my friends I had known since sixth grade," she says.

"Sophomore year? Sheesh. Bad timing for sure." I could feel her pain.

"I was angry. So I sulked. I had no choice but to accept the move and get over it," she said.

Surprisingly, things went better than expected. On her first day at the new school, she ran into a guy whom she knew from the old one. He introduced her to a group of girls he thought she'd like, and she did. The three girls quickly became her best friends. And while she says it was scary at first being the new kid, she was thankful to have found the best friends a girl could have. And it worked out, mostly.

At the same time, another group of girls befriended her as well. These girls were a curious bunch of African American girls who wanted to know everything about Dibora because she looked like an Ethiopian classmate they knew.

"Of course, I told them I am Ethiopian, and that clicked with them at first," she says. "They even liked me."

But the difference was that these girls were first-generation African Americans whose parents had immigrated to the United States from various African countries and tribes. Tribal culture was still being practiced in their homes, a tricky concept to understand. So when Dibora's six-foot-six white dad showed up one day, wandering the halls of the school to find her after cross-country practice, white dad didn't click with the girls. In fact, the girls had never heard of adoption. Dibora says they couldn't believe she belonged to a white family.

"They thought my dad was someone helping out my family. He's tall and Dutch, and I'm short and Ethiopian."

She says her new African friends didn't know what to say. They must have talked about her that night, because the next day things changed.

Standing around the lockers, a girl teased Dibora.

"So you have white on the inside and black on the outside? You're an Oreo," the girl mocked.

"How did you handle it?" I ask.

At first she played along. "Ha! Very funny." She remembers responding sarcastically. All the kids gathered around laughed and called her Oreo too. It cut Dibora to the core, but it didn't stop at one and done. The name calling went on for months. She continued to brush it off. Over time, however, she says, "I secretly seethed inside."

Dibora couldn't understand why these girls' perception of her had changed just because she was being raised in a white family.

"I was so hurt. I told them they were acting like five-year-olds."

But it was no use. She even threatened to tell their teachers, but that didn't work either. The angrier she got, the more it egged them on. She said they continued calling her Oreo through her sophomore year and into her junior year.

"How strange that these kids were so weirded out," I say.

"Yeah, I didn't know how to get them to stop."

That is, until her junior year prom night.

Dibora and her best friends were getting dressed in one of their bedrooms, which overflowed with makeup, frilly dresses, and laughter.

"I had borrowed my dress from my sister, who had recently been a bridesmaid in a wedding."

Breaking from tradition, Dibora chose a short, flowy,

pinkish-purple dress and wore sparkly, strappy stilettos that, she confessed, hurt her feet so badly she couldn't stand it. While the girls snacked on Mexican food and brownies, Dibora styled everyone's hair. Before they took off to the dance at a local country club, they posed for pictures.

"When I look back at those pictures now, the night seems bittersweet."

"Why?" I dare to ask.

"At the country club, I kicked off my shoes and we hit the dance floor," Dibora says.

The DJ was thumping. Teens grinding.

"I don't grind. It's gross. I don't want some strange guy rubbing on me."

She requested a slow, romantic song: "Thinking Out Loud," by Ed Sheeran.

"I love that song," she says. "It was my prom too, right?"

When the girls who'd bullied her on a regular basis saw her dancing to an Ed Sheeran song, they moved in.

"Look at her, she dances like a white girl and listens to white people's songs!"

"Seriously?" I whisper.

Her friends stood next to her like a shield. Then from the other group, one girl with a serious glare got in Dibora's face. "We don't claim you anymore!"

That's when Dibora leaned in, barefoot and all, and yelled, "Tribes claim people. You are not my tribe. Nobody claims me. I am just as African as you."

She had reached the end of her rope.

"But I wasn't afraid. I wasn't shaking."

She says she broke out in a sweat though.

"I let it all out in one big breath."

The DJ pushed pause on the music. The dancing stopped. Teachers surrounded the small group of girls and watched and waited to see where it would go. Dibora exploded. "No one but my *real* friends, my family, and most importantly God, claims me!"

This was beginning to sound like the next *Footloose* movie, I thought.

Then she took another deep breath and walked away. Dibora had stood up for herself.

The next school day, the girls involved stopped calling her Oreo, and she was thankful. But did they know how much they had hurt her?

"Did they know I lost my first family? Did they know being adopted hasn't been a walk in the park? Did they know that my birth parents left me on my own to take care of a three-year-old and a newborn and scavenge for food? I was five. I still try to parent my little brother today. If God had not been with us, I would not have survived. I lived in two different orphanages, and it was very scary. I remember strange men taking care of a bunch of kids. Three kids slept together in small beds. It smelled disgusting. The food was gross, the rooms were never clean, and all the kids were crammed together in a small space. Nobody expected us to get adopted from that place.

"No kid should have to go through that. I had to grow up very quickly."

Then one day, she and her brother were moved to Hannah's Hope. It had a school and playground and good food. When the civil war spread, Dibora and her brother were some of the last kids to be adopted.

"One day we were on the playground and the next on a plane

to America. I had to learn to be a kid and play again. For the longest time, I didn't feel like I belonged. Forever, I will struggle with not knowing my birth parents or seeing who I look like most. Did those mean girls know?"

Now it was my turn to take a deep breath. Dibora is my hero, a young Ethiopian American adopted person not afraid to stand up for herself. She is proud of who she is and of her adoptive family too. She hasn't chosen the trajectory of her life, yet she chose to embrace it and believe in herself. Being a grown-up means becoming more, not less. And that night at the prom, Dibora didn't tolerate the status quo of injustice.

" STAND STRONG IN WHO YOU ARE. . . . IT'S YOUR STORY.

I ask her to share advice for teens who find themselves in her shoes. She confidently says, "Don't be surprised if kids in school don't understand adoption or don't get it that you have parents who look different than you. Stand strong in who you are. Don't be embarrassed about your adoption. It's your story. There will never be enough words to explain adoption. Believe in yourself."

Sometimes you choose your friends, and sometimes they choose you. I recently discovered a quote about friendship from people smarter than me. They say, "Your friends will give shape to your life. They will either stunt your growth or spur you on. And when you find good friends, keep them. They are like gold. Treasure them. Invest in them. Spur them on too. Be the kind of friend that you would like to have."[1]

CHAPTER 4

WHO AM I?

I am leaving you with a gift—peace of mind and heart.
And the peace I give is a gift the world cannot give.

JOHN 14:27 (NLT)

IF EVER THERE was a guy who seemed to have it all together, Derek is that guy. In high school, he showed up for every tryout and audition and team. Enter his house through the garage and the floor would be littered with cleats—football cleats, soccer cleats, golf cleats, running cleats, not to mention black dress shoes for choir performances, and a pair or two of Chaco's for hiking or the beach. Derek fit in everywhere and got along with everyone.

But he says while he was living a pretty solid teen life, inside he was mystified by a relentless ache he couldn't put into words. It seemed that no matter how many teams and clubs he joined— he says he had a blast and learned a lot—he didn't feel like he'd ever really belong, and he couldn't shake the feeling. The question "Who am I?" lay just beneath the surface, along with an edgy need to search constantly for some sense of self.

"I just wanted to belong somewhere people wanted and valued me," Derek tells me over FaceTime from Colorado.

While other kids were binge-watching *The Office*, Derek was finding something new to do. He figures it was his way of finding himself. Like the time he tried out for Pirate No. 3 in the swash-buckling romantic musical comedy *Pirates of Penzance*.

"Why the pirate musical?" I ask.

"I had a decent voice and could grow a black beard on my own at sixteen." He laughs, and so do I. "And being chased by pretty girls was a good gig for a guy to have," he adds with a smile.

Derek is now twenty-five. He's married and hopelessly in love, a rookie business professional, and a happy guy. He was adopted by his parents at birth. He says his adoption was open from the start.

"I knew my birth mom and her family. I never felt like she abandoned me. It wasn't until I was ten that I realized I had two moms. At the time, it made sense to me. I didn't think it was weird at all. There was no tension or strain . . . although, having two moms was weird when I didn't know what to call my moms if they were in the same room. 'Hey you!'" He laughs. "In that situation, my mom could sense the extra tension. I was generally cuddly and gave a lot of hugs. But when the other family was around, I was less huggy."

Knowing his birth origin and connecting with his birth mom should have helped Derek sort out his inner turmoil. And maybe it did, a little. But as he grew into his body and beard, he got angry. Not because he was adopted, he says, but because he couldn't figure out who he was. Which is common for teens, but Derek says it was something more; somewhere in the depths of his being, it felt like a bomb was about to explode.

"Thinking back on it, maybe that's why I jumped into so many sports and clubs and musicals. Maybe I was searching for something to release the internal pressure I felt building up. I felt like I couldn't be myself, so if I could be everything to everyone, I'd satisfy my inner conflict."

Derek says he spent a lot of energy struggling to find his fit in this world—the timeless "Who am I?" search. But as a teen, Derek didn't associate his struggle with his separation from his birth mother. We consider the possibility.

"Could there be a link?" I ask.

"At the time, I did not know the two were related. But I think they were," he admits.

He adds, "I wanted an identity of my own so badly that when I couldn't figure it out, I went searching. And when I found a place to belong, like on a sports team, I still felt unsettled. It was a constant battle that led me to become one angry guy. The only people who knew or sensed I was angry, other than my parents, were my teammates. People knew I could get pretty fiery. People could feel that negative vibe, and it wasn't passion for the game. It was anger. In middle school and in high school, I had anger issues. I had some sort of agitation."

"'Agitation' says it so well," I agree. "How did you handle it?"

"I didn't handle it well in some cases," Derek says. "I did not have the capacity as a kid to handle it appropriately. I knew it was okay to be angry, but I didn't know how to manage it as a young kid or teen. Oh, I tried. I'd rather try my best than not try at all. I do better now that I am older."

"Did you speak about your anger to a therapist?" I ask somewhat carefully.

"In ninth grade I talked to a therapist because I didn't like the way I felt. I went two or three times, and he only made me feel angrier."

"Not to diss therapy."

"No. I was too young. At the time, I didn't know what to do with therapy. It worked better for me when I would talk to other mentors, like my parents' friends, who allowed me to connect with them when I needed them."

Derek says a bunch of people tried to pour into him, but it was his dad who helped him most. His dad was his closest ally, who kept reaching out and tossing him lifeline after lifeline, trying to help him sort out the inner chaos.

"He was your sounding board?" I ask.

"Yes. My dad and I talked about emotions and spiritual things while exercising. We would run together for three to six miles while I was practicing for cross-country. Or he would bike with me when I was training for a marathon. We'd talk about who God is, what Scripture means, why it matters, and how we should apply it. These long talks helped me gain a spiritual view of the world. We also talked about emotions. It was key having a male role model talk to me about emotions. He's my best friend. He was my best man in my wedding."

"You two really connected," I say, cherishing the thought of Derek and his dad standing side by side during the most important day of his life.

"Yeah! Somehow, he could see what I couldn't see. Over the years, he tried to help me disarm the ticking bomb inside. He said it's okay to wonder and not know who you are all at once. It is a process and a part of growing up."

We talk about his approach to finding himself, the bingeing on clubs and teams and plays. He says he was glad he had gotten involved in all that stuff rather than vaping, drugs, drinking or tanking in school.

"At least the skills I got from trying everything helped me develop and build healthy connections with people," he says. "A lot of teens dabble in short-term distractions that lead nowhere. Vaping is not a skill."

After high school, like all kids, Derek had to choose his next move: go to college, get a job, join the military, or take a gap year. He chose the gap year, then applied at and was accepted by Youth with a Mission, a Christian organization that trains teens to serve underserved populations in third-world countries. It wasn't a gap year, more like a gap five months, but he says it changed his life forever.

"I thought, Why not?, packed my bags and my anger and frustrations, and hopped on a plane to New Zealand for three months of training, then to Cambodia to serve. For two months we cared for kids on the streets."

Things got real in Cambodia. Confronted with the needs of lost children on the streets one night, alone in his room, exhausted and emotionally spent, Derek confronted God about life, where hope comes from, and ultimately, his identity.

"I don't get it," I say. "How did you go from serving in the streets to this huge confrontation about who you are? Can you explain what happened?"

"In the moment, there was a lot of real emotion," Derek explains. "I was alone on a roof looking over a city in pain. I felt my soul connect with the pain, and yet I knew I had something more in my heart. All the anger just exploded. I cried. I wanted answers. I demanded answers. Who am I? Where does my hope come from? Why should I have hope? Why am I here? It was like I was throwing a fit using all of my angry questions as punches. I wrestled for hours with these thoughts. Finally, I was spent; having totally emptied every complaint I ever had about myself into the air, I collapsed into the biggest bear hug by the biggest Being in the universe, and God was gracious and allowed me peace. I slept that night deeper than I ever had before."

"So let me get this straight. You unleashed an explosion of questions and pain and words that didn't make sense, and from that you felt peace?"

"Yeah. It wasn't like I received divine answers. I don't know how to explain it or describe it. I didn't feel like everything got better. But I was granted peace in that moment. Peace was my answer. And peace has made all the difference in who I am today."

"Anger gone?"

"Not gone. It's always under the surface, but now I appreciate it. Having that experience was a pivotal point. That's when I changed. Knowing peace gave me something to give to others. When I went to college, I was a different person."

❝❝ GOD WAS NOT INTIMIDATED BY MY CONFUSION OR ANGST.

"So you're saying you wrestled with God and a shift took place?"

"Yes. God was not intimidated by my confusion or angst. He was just waiting until I took time to take him seriously."

I smile. "Or to throw the first punch?"

"I definitely threw the first punch," Derek answers. "I initiated it. He was waiting for me to do it. Even if it comes from anger, he's not scared. He's ready for anything. Some people have to be called out of their slumber. Others, he meets you where you're at, like me. Some people won't understand this, but if they can get to God sooner than I did, it will make their life better—not easier, but better."

"Scripture is full of these wrestling matches," I point out. "Any ground rules?"

"In the moment, no! I just started swinging. Total free-for-all. But this is important. After I got off my chest what I thought I needed to, a few days later I was ready to listen and waited for God to connect with me. Both sides should have equal fighting time. God will not lash out or hit you hard after you lash out. He will allow you to be honest and vulnerable. But if you want the fullness of it, you have to be ready to listen to his honest response. We have to be prepared to hear his small whisper and not wait for a grand revelation. Hearing God comes with constant listening.

"Putting words to what was going on inside my heart wasn't easy," he continues. "I cried it out . . . no, yelled it out. Putting my feelings into words was a huge step toward defusing the bomb."

"So, you're not the first angry, adopted teen to take this journey to find peace," I say. "But you may be the first to confess that at eighteen you duked it out with God for answers. Do you recommend this route, this holy catharsis, to other teens?"

He laughs. "Emotions are real and should be appreciated. But they should be used like tools; we use them, they don't control us. No matter how mixed up or shaken you are by life, remember these truths: God allows you to encourage and be encouraged by those around you. Keep moving forward no matter how you feel. Find healthy ways to explore your identity. Don't fall for short-term distractions that undermine your self-worth; actions have consequences.

"Maybe teens think if they ignore their emotions, they won't have to face whatever is ticking away in their own heart. I could have been one of those teens, searching through junk to find myself. But I chose to wrestle it out and listen to the One who gives peace and purpose. He settled my soul."

Sometimes we need space and distance from everyday life to see things with new eyes. And it is absolutely okay to wrestle with God and process your mixed-up emotions out loud . . . emphasis on the loud. When I need some one on one with God, my go-to is Scripture, especially the Psalms in the Old Testament. If you are questioning, wondering, angry, weak, lost, that's the place to meet with God, and he will soothe your soul. God *wants* to hear from you, whether it's good, bad, or ugly. Get wrestling!

CHAPTER 5

MAKING PROGRESS

A ship in harbor is safe,
but that is not what ships are built for.

JOHN A. SHEDD

ANXIETY HAD A firm hold on Sophia from the beginning, but today this college student has a better hold on it. It wasn't easy. She resisted help for sure. But every "yes" she had to dig for helped her grow. So, what if progress is loaded with ups and downs? What if resistance tries to block the way forward? What if forward isn't always straight? What if saying yes over and over adds up to something better over time like it did for Sophia?

Sophia's birth name was Karla Elaina Gonzalez Pineda. Named after Karl Marx, she was told, which I found odd and interesting—to be named after the father of communism. She's Sophia today. She was born in Guatemala, one of seven children relinquished by her birth mother. At the orphanage, Sophia toddled around with kids her age who looked like her until she was almost two. That's when her single mom, a sweet and spicy Italian in her fifties, adopted her, and the twosome settled in Brooklyn, New York. It was a whole new world.

The pair lived in a seven-hundred-square-foot second-story apartment, perfect for two, near trendy Prospect Park, restaurants, coffee shops, and Manhattan. Sophia grew up giggling and baking with her mom in their narrow, compact galley kitchen, which was barely big enough for two. They played board games on the area rug covering the vintage parquet floor. Life happened in this sweet, small space: sleepovers, movie nights, homework, and crazy dancing with her cat, Dumplin. Home was the hub of love and support and all that was good. To the casual observer nothing seemed out of place, but for those who knew, Sophia lived with anxiety that interfered from the beginning.

"My mom always said I was an anxious kid since the day she adopted me," Sophia fills me in. "I would cry for no reason and pace back and forth when I was able to walk. I was always on alert. The first year I was with her, I wouldn't fall asleep unless I was in her arms or beside her in her bed."

Today, at twenty-one, she's a 4.0 college student bouncing around between majors, trying to figure out what she wants to do. She's creative and dabbles in designing graphics for T-shirts and mugs for her online side hustle, dresses like a New York City girl, says she's shy until she knows someone, and is outgoing once she does.

So, what was going on with Sophia? Why so much anxiety while she was growing up? Sophia had an overwhelming fear of being abandoned again. So despite growing up secure in her cozy childhood home with her rock-star mom, she battled an underlying feeling of loneliness and worry ever since she can remember.

Being away from her mom didn't feel safe. Day care was impossible, too scary. By three she was in play therapy. Even in middle school, she was never able to be far away from her mom for even a night.

"I hated sleepovers until I was thirteen unless they were at my house. I started sleeping in my own bed without my mom in the room around age sixteen, but it was scary at first."

"Therapy has helped tremendously," she admits, totally opening up. "I've been in therapy since I was three. It made me feel less alone."

Looking back, her mom's encouragement, good schools, and therapy were game changers, but overcoming anxiety was not an overnight success story. I'm not sure it ever is. Sophia had plenty of setbacks throughout the years. Partly, she didn't always accept that she needed outside help, especially when she needed it most.

So when her anxiety escalated in high school for various reasons, her mom encouraged her to spend the summer between her junior and senior year at a residential mental health treatment academy for teens. There she could learn new strategies to manage her anxiety. The stay would gobble up her summer. The suggestion didn't sit well at first. She was seventeen going on eighteen and had to make a choice. Naturally, she resisted. Most teenagers would.

"You went?" I said.

"Yes. I didn't want to go there."

"But you did it?"

"Yes. Once I was there, I at least wanted to try to learn to control my anxiety better."

"You made progress?"

"Some."

Sophia had said yes to an opportunity. And, settled in at the academy, for the next six weeks she was surrounded by lush green landscape. She worked in the vegetable gardens and enjoyed fresh air—a big change from Brooklyn. That part she liked. She quickly found out that some sessions she attended were better than others. All in all, she picked up some new strategies, had a nasty panic attack while she was there, and muscled through. None of it was ideal. It wasn't intended to be a Disney vacation but, rather, a place where she could learn coping strategies and how to modify her thoughts and behaviors. It had been difficult. Not everything is easy. Sometimes our greatest growth comes when persevering through hard things.

When the six weeks were up, Sophia was matched with a therapist that specializes in her kind of anxiety.

"It's going well."

She says it's by far the best fit.

Around this same time, while she was making progress with her anxiety episodes, her mom was diagnosed with cancer. Months of doctor visits and uncertainty about her mom's illness nudged Sophia to do something she had wanted to do for a long time: search for her birth family.

"All my life I had wanted to know more. It was like a blank page in my life. I would write letters to send to my birth mom, but I would never send them. I thought with my mom having cancer, finding them would give me another family. I wanted to have my mom there when I was doing the search."

With her mom's blessing, she went for it.

It didn't take long for Sophia to find two birth siblings in the US.

"You're no longer an only child," I say with a smile.

"I know. I was afraid I'd be alone if my mom died of cancer. The whole blood relation thing is comforting. Something about it feels comfortable and right. It's one connection I have that I didn't have growing up. I like it. I like knowing."

After finding two of seven birth siblings on a Guatemala

adoptee Facebook group, she discovered her older brother was in contact with their birth mother in Guatemala. Once again she said yes, this time to a deeply personal connection. She admits she was nervous, and it felt awkward when she first met her birth mother over FaceTime. It was bittersweet. She kept her expectations in check.

"One of my worst fears was that my birth mother didn't think about me or care where I ended up."

"Did she?"

"When I spoke to her, she said that she thought about me all the time and hoped I was okay."

"That had to mean a lot."

"I thought it would mean everything to me. It was nice to know. But it didn't change much. It didn't change the fact she put me up for adoption, where I spent my life feeling lost and confused. At that point, she wasn't my mom anymore. She was a stranger to me, but I will always care about her and think of her."

She thought about it some more and offered this insight: "When you think about looking for your birth mother, think about what you can give to her, like relief. In a way, it gives her a chance to heal too."

After reconnecting with her birth siblings and finding her birth mother, Sophia's anxiety episodes didn't spontaneously disappear. But learning the truth about her birth story reassured her sense of self and she found closure. She says she talks to her older brother in the army in South Carolina on a regular basis.

In the spring of that following year, Sophia's sweet and saucy Italian mom, her best friend and encourager, died of cancer. She was seventy-three. Sophia was just finishing up her first year of college. No matter how well her mom had prepared her—they had talked for hours and hours about what was next—Sophia wasn't prepared. In that season of grieving, I watched her Instagram light up. Posting was her outlet and one way to welcome family and friends into her sorrow. They hovered close, answering her posts; I joined them. We all offered encouragement, prayers, and hope.

Months later she told me about the dainty cross she wears around her neck. She said, "I believe that God has a plan for all of us and that God watches over everyone so that no one is ever alone."

She grieved deeply. Then, slowly, I saw a change. The leaves were changing colors. She was posting happy pictures of the little changes she was making to her tiny, cozy apartment she grew up in, celebrating her birthday and her mom's too, taking selfies outdoors with her fiancé, and adopting more animals, like Coconut the rabbit and Dizzie, a white terrier. She was coming back! And as a deeper thinker with a stronger sense of self, a young woman with hope and a future.

> **PROGRESS HAPPENS WHEN YOU'RE INTENTIONAL . . . BUT SOMETIMES PROGRESS LOOKS LIKE ONE STEP FORWARD AND TWO STEPS BACKWARD.**

"I never gave up when things felt impossible," she says. "I believe that every obstacle we face helps to shape us into what we were meant to be, and they make us strong." As for her anxiety episodes, whether she is aging out of her fears or practicing the coping tools she's learned in therapy over the years, or all the above, Sophia says it's less and less triggered. At twenty-one, she barely notices her anxiety.

Is Sophia a poster child for progress? If there is such a thing, I'd say yes. Her progress isn't perfect. Nobody perfects progress. It is something we just have to do. Somewhere I read that progress is definite but difficult; progress isn't always smooth. Progress happens when you're intentional, especially when you want to make your way forward to achieve a specific goal, such as learning to control anxiety like Sophia did.

But sometimes progress looks like one step forward and two steps backward. It's a tricky endeavor. When I read between the lines of her story, I notice her reluctant yes. Even if it was reluctant, it was a good yes, a moving forward kind of yes.

What if saying yes helped her grow? Every yes added up. Her yes to therapy. Her yes to a summer at a wellness academy, and so on. What if every yes means more trust . . . and more trust means less fear . . . over and over again until you break through. Think of all the breakthroughs throughout this book. Many started with a shaky, resistant "Yes, I'll try it." Breakthroughs don't just happen in a moment but over years, through mini-breakthroughs and digging for the yes.

CHAPTER 6

BAKE IT 'TIL YOU MAKE IT

This is my invariable advice to people:
learn how to cook—try new recipes, learn from your mistakes,
be fearless, and above all have fun!

JULIA CHILD

MEET ME AT my shop," she texted. I expect to arrive at a boutique bakery in a small corner of the city, the kind with floor to ceiling plate glass windows that lure you in with lovely silver trays and white tiers of carefully stacked cakes and other culinary confections. My taste buds are watering for a homemade macaron, and hers are the best.

Instead, the address I tell Siri brings me to an upscale active-living retirement community, the type that oozes luxury inside and out of its towering grand doorway that leads to nothing but surprises.

"Some shop," I laugh when I enter, taken in by the forty-foot ceilings which soar above me and the highly polished granite floors under my feet. Have I just stepped on board an elegant cruise ship moored in port? Annie comes to me, arms stretching wide, and greets me with a lingering hug. She's twenty-nine, a beautiful, petite African American woman, barely a size two, wearing a professional, crisp white chef's apron over a soft long-sleeve top, black slacks, and flats. Her hair is elegantly pulled back with a floral print scarf.

"Are you a pastry chef here?" I ask, my eyes scanning the large foyer, the staff, the brightly lit deli with quaint café tables and chairs. She smiles and fills me in as she guides me to a table away from the café where we can talk.

"Yes," she says. I can tell she's in her element. I order a salad and she orders a wrap. This section is served by uniformed wait staff that fuss over Annie. I quickly get the impression she is a VIP. Anyone who creates pastries and breads is a VIP in my book.

"So this is your shop?" I ask, gesturing with my hands to the grand elegance, pinning her with a curious grin.

"Actually, I design dessert menus and create unique desserts and breads for four boutique restaurants here. I am contracted as an executive pastry chef. The position was created just for me by the executive chef."

"I had no idea." *Impressive*, I say to myself.

She tells me how the chef took her under his wing and sent her to training at various places, which helped her grow as a pastry chef. My salad and her wrap arrive, and we stop briefly to take our first bite.

"So how did this all begin?" I ask.

"I had a huge sweet tooth as a kid. My mom and grandma baked a lot, and that's what started it. I always wanted to lick the batter-covered beaters. One day I figured out that if I learned to bake myself, I could lick the beaters all the time."

"Ha! Smart."

Annie was adopted as an infant into a large family. She was seven when she first learned how to use the oven. I was too. But we both know times have change.

She laughs. "Today, most parents wouldn't allow their young kids near a hot oven."

The kitchen became her refuge.

"I come from a large family of seven kids, all of us domestically adopted. Plus we fostered even more kids and homeschooled. With all the commotion and sharing my room with complete strangers who came and went, I felt lost."

Annie found peace in the kitchen.

"My parents were frazzled, and it showed, at least at home. Outside our house, we looked squeaky clean. Inside, we were a hot mess. Baking became my escape from the chaos and a way to be creative."

Annie checks her timer and excuses herself to check on the ovens in the main kitchen. I'm left to my imagination: a stressed-out young girl, flour-filled bowls, measuring cups in motion, a pinch of this and that. I fork my greens. Annie returns to our table. She tells me she will return to the kitchen shortly to check again.

"So you're saying as a little girl, baking helped?" I asked between bites.

"Yes."

Later, I check out the link between baking and stress. It turns out, according to a slew of articles written by experts, that baking can reduce anxiety, stress, and depression.[2] I thought about Annie losing herself in a recipe, measuring with precision, adding a drop of this and a pinch of that while the rest of the world disappeared.

"At ten, I entered my first baking contest: an apple pie contest at Klackle Orchards. My mom signed me up for the kids-twelve-and-under contest."

Annie remembers red-and-white-checkered tablecloths covered with pies when they arrived. She set hers next to the others.

"I definitely didn't think I would win. But I did—first place!

"My flakey crust stood out to the judges, plus I had sliced my apples really thin. The spices were not measured but sprinkled to taste and from memory. I cried when I held my first blue ribbon and a cash prize, but winning meant so much more than that. This was a turning point that gave me confidence I didn't have before."

Trying and failing and figuring out recipes shaped Annie to be competitive and push herself for the first time.

"I had found something of my very own."

Annie continued baking at home. It gave her purpose and peace. She also hung out at the neighborhood Dutch bakery surrounded by shelves of fresh apple fritters; cinnamon and sprinkle donuts; rye, wheat, and sourdough breads; and her favorite—warm, chocolate-glazed cinnamon rolls. Sitting where she could see, she'd sneak peeks at production in the back: warm bread on trays coming from hot ovens, cookies being decorated with colorful icing, and donut glazing.

"Now that I am older, I look back and see that I had my mind set on being a pastry chef from a young age."

So when the bakery owner offered her a job—she was a serious regular—she snagged it. Behind the glass counter, she boxed donuts, bagged fresh breads, worked the cash register, and cleaned in between.

"I loved my job. It was heaven, and so much fun. I worked there all through high school."

The summer she turned eighteen, before going to culinary school, she attended a baking event in the city. While waiting in line to get in, a stranger introduced her to Marge, owner of the iconic Marge's Donut Den on the southwest side of town. It was like meeting a celebrity from *Cake Wars* on Food Network. The two talked, and before Annie knew it, Marge offered her a job working the counter at her shop. She says she freaked out so much that she put her plans for culinary school on hold.

"This was a chance I couldn't miss," she says.

Soon after Annie pulled on her apron, Marge asked her to head to the back, into the kitchen, and decorate a cake. She tells me she thought it was a test or something.

"I didn't know what I was doing. I picked up my tools and began frosting the cake in white, then added green vines with yellow buds."

She continues.

"The cake sold in ten minutes! After that, I never worked the front counter again."

She says creating wedding cakes was nerve wracking and intimidating. The bride's glowing smile of approval meant everything to her. Cupcakes were super fun too. She remembers a time a high school boy came in to order a cupcake with a special message to his girlfriend: Will you be my prom date? It was so romantic. Creativity oozed from her piping bag. She knew she was made for this. People liked her pastries, and they liked her too. She felt affirmed.

"It sounds like you've come a long way from that little lost girl trying to find her way in the kitchen?" I ask.

"I have," she replies, checks her timer and heads back to the kitchen to check the bread.

She says baking gave her a place where she felt like she belonged, and it kept her anxiety in check. She says training with Marge was such a God gift because she soon figured out she's a hands-on girl and suspects she may have gone crazy in a culinary-school setting. Who knows?

Annie returns from the kitchen with a large white bag and sets it aside.

"Earlier you mentioned the chaos in your family and finding refuge in the kitchen. A lot of good stuff has happened since then."

"Yes. I am so glad I found myself in spite of the challenging years at home. But I worked at it. I am so thankful the right, good people saw my potential and gave me a chance. But I chose to listen. I was so determined to make it as a pastry chef that I wasn't afraid to work my way through the ranks, pay my dues, and work hard."

"Any advice to others who may have a challenging home life like you did?"

"Be open to being coached and taught and tutored. Do not lose yourself in social media and the fake, the edited, the unauthentic. Don't self-medicate; self-elevate. Try doing something with your hands—art, music, making furniture, sewing, cooking, horseback riding. For me, I found creating something with my hands meant everything. I learned how to figure things out, fix mistakes, and dig in and research what I needed to know, all life skills that can never be taken away."

"You're married now?"

"Yes. My husband and I just bought a fixer-upper in the country with some land."

"Chickens and gardens in your future?"

"I think so. We'll have to learn."

"That seems to be your theme."

She leans over, picks up the white bag, and offers it to me with a big smile. Taking it in my hands, I quickly feel the weight of something warm. I reach inside and lift a fresh-baked savory herb bread to my nose, a signature loaf Annie created.

"You know this isn't going to make it home," I say with a silly smile on my face. Bread is my love language.

She laughs.

> **FIND SOMETHING THAT YOU LOVE AND THAT YOU ARE GOOD AT AND SET YOUR HEART ON IT. MAKE IT YOURS.**

She left me with a warm hug and a warm loaf of bread and a warm thought for you.

"Find something that you love and that you are good at and set your heart on it. Make it yours. Mine is baking. What's yours?"

You may not be a baker like Annie, but that doesn't mean you can't find your sweet spot. Sometimes you find yourself through trial and error. Baking, wood carving, sound and lighting crew for the high school musical, bike repair, sports, robotics . . . find something that takes you somewhere new and outside your emotional life. When you coax your focus to something new, good things happen. Your mind fills with creativity, innovation, and accomplishment while crowding out insecurities and lack of self-worth.

CHAPTER 7

RESOLVE TO FORGIVE

It is not the strength of the body that counts, but the strength of the spirit.

J. R. R. TOLKIEN

I WAS BORN to a sixteen-year-old girl who already had an eighteen-month-old son by the time she was thirteen. My mom was already an alcoholic and a druggie by then. She was hooked on cocaine and drank while she was pregnant with me."

Amelia doesn't tiptoe around. She had a rough go from the start. Fetal alcohol spectrum disorder (FASD), prenatal exposure to cocaine, abuse, and neglect. No child should have a résumé like this. It's safe to say that if her mom hadn't been using and drinking, Amelia and her siblings would have been healthy babies.

"To this day, she [mom] says our diagnoses are fake and lies," Amelia says. "It frustrates me that she denies it. It is what it is, and there's not much we can do about it."

Amelia is twenty-one. She's a happy introvert who enjoys hanging out with her family and friends. But like most introverts, people and parties tend to drain her energy after a while. Extroverts are energized by people; introverts get drained, like a battery that needs to be recharged. So when she's had enough of her überlarge, supercharged family, she's on the couch with a good book, like the Lord of the Rings series or fan fiction.

Amelia was only three the first time she, her older brother, and her younger sister were moved to foster care. It took years of shuttling back and forth between her foster family and her mom until she was finally, happily, thankfully, and officially adopted by her foster family when she turned eight. She's now one of eleven kids. Four of them are her blood siblings, four are the birth kids, and two were adopted from Ethiopia. They are an amazing collection of kids, a real family with real family challenges, and unique ones as well. Most of the adopted kids suffer from FASD, reactive attachment disorder, ADHD, and prenatal exposure to drugs. In fact, when I met with Amelia, she told me one younger sister had just returned from an extended stay at a school in Arizona because she suffers from reactive attachment disorder—or, said differently, the whole family suffers from her violent outbursts. All the kids have been or are currently home-schooled by their mom. They've also grown up running free in wide-open fields blanketed with wild daisies, tending farm critters, and in the recent past, raising rabbits for show—hundreds of them.

Amelia smiles trying to recall the names of one hundred rabbits. *Seriously?* I think to myself. Many had names, she says. How you tell one bunny from another is out of my league.

We had decided to meet at a local restaurant known for its pizza and mile-high nachos. The restaurant is situated in a college town about a forty-minute drive for me and a fifteen-minute drive from Amelia's family farm, which she says is in the middle of nowhere. She arrives in an older-model, silver Buick sedan—a family car, I gather—with one of her sisters in the passenger seat. Amelia is five foot four with short black hair, of Hispanic descent. She is wearing a cool new pair of thick, bluish purple–rimmed glasses and an infectious smile. Her sister, Victoria, is a peanut, a smiley wisp of a teen with a warmer skin tone than her sister's. Tori appears to be about fifteen. We head inside to a booth and slide in.

It's two in the afternoon, and we have the place practically to ourselves. Amelia glances up from her menu. Our server drops off three waters and straws and takes our order.

Amelia's wrists, neck, and earlobes are draped in an eclectic collection of metals, leather, dangles and sparkles. Across the booth, I notice her rubbing her thumb along the rough edges of her faux diamond–studded leather bracelet. She catches me watching her.

"It helps me relax," she says, then explains that her jewelry masquerades as sensory fidgets: a place to land her hand and fingers in order to calm her nerves or relieve a sudden tremor in her right arm that could occur at any time. All because she was exposed to drugs in the womb.

"I have random tremors," she tells me. "Could be from prenatal exposure to cocaine. My doctors are surprised I don't have seizures."

Colorful, textured bracelets circle her wrist, and one in particular has an image of a wolf carved into black leather. Wolves are her favorite animal, she says, next to whales and rabbits. She shifts focus to her fingers, which are filled with a collection of rings she's either bought, found, or stolen from her sister. With a slightly smug grin, she peeks at Tori to her right. They catch each other's eyes and burst out laughing. Apparently they take each other's belongings a lot without asking.

A basket of fried cheese sticks arrives. The girls take a moment to negotiate who will get the ranch dipping sauce and who will take the marinara. It all happens in a blink of an eye and without drama. It's obvious these two are close friends.

While Amelia settles in, her hand subtly moves from one piece of jewelry to the next, stealthily rubbing the textures. She's quick to bring me up to speed that all four of her birth siblings have FASD. I grit my teeth. The pile of research on prenatal exposure to alcohol is conclusive: we're talking about a spectrum of birth defects that negatively impact growth, coordination, and sensory processing, and create intellectual disabilities. All preventable if the mother doesn't drink alcohol.

Amelia points to her sister's face while she's eating a fried cheese stick. "She's the only one with FASD facial features; a small nose, small eye openings, et cetera." Her finger circles her sister's face like a guide on a tour bus pointing out the sites. Again, the girls laugh. Tori casually agrees—"Yep"—like it's no big deal, and continues crunching away, listening with one ear tuned to us while checking Instagram. Neither girl could care less about their labels, but both are very aware of what is going on. Or more specifically, what's gone wrong.

The mile-high nachos arrive at our table. Amelia's fingers carefully dodge the sour cream and pick up a chip covered in taco meat immersed in gooey, golden cheese.

"I'm on the lower end of the spectrum, thank God," she says.

"I am thankful too," I say, smiling and shaking my head in disbelief. Her attitude moves me; she's thankful, not hateful. It's unexpected.

From what I gather from Amelia, all her birth siblings have learning disabilities that make some things, like algebra or catching balls, harder than they should be. Amelia hates math. It doesn't make sense. But what does make sense is reading, especially if it's a four-hundred-page Tolkien novel.

Tori looks up from her plate and grins. "I love math!" The sisters banter a bit about their love-hate relationship with math, talking about what comes easy and what type of problems they like doing, and then move on. Amelia tells me she's forgetful and has trouble completing tasks without a nudge—or two or three or four. That's attention deficit disorder (ADD), an inability to attend to tasks. I've also heard it described as if the traffic cop that controls the brain is off duty a lot, bellied up to a coffee bar and eating donuts, unaffected unless it's an emergency.

Amelia says her attention to detail has gotten better as she's gotten older. So has her lack of hand-eye coordination. Growing up, any sport that involved catching, throwing, or kicking a ball was a disaster.

I love that she is living proof that time and maturity help.

Then unexpectedly, between bites an old memory surfaces. "When I was in middle school, my parents had to fight with me to take a shower. Back then, I didn't like getting my hair wet. But once I was in, I'd take really long showers. Thankfully, I'm over it," she proclaims.

She reminisces about how messed up her sensory system was back then. Tori jumps in and adds, "Things were messed up when I was processing too."

Amelia shoots her an amused look. "What? Processing? What are you, bologna?"

When I finally figure out they are talking about processing in the womb, like bologna processes in the meat plant, we are all laughing. If such a thing exists, these two could do stand-up comedy about FASD.

While the girls make light of their diagnoses, they are also articulate and thoughtful. It is clear FASD doesn't define them. Then Amelia shares a story about the neglect she endured as a little kid. She sets her nacho down, more serious now.

"I don't remember an awful lot about the first three years of my life, but I remember to some extent the abuse I suffered. We didn't have a routine. Waking up in the morning, we wondered what would happen every day. She, Mom, was always drunk. Once she was so drunk, we even got kicked out of a homeless shelter. I remember one time my stepdad had been at a party, drinking. He came home drunk out of his mind. He comes into the room while my older brother and I are sleeping and slaps us across the face with his huge leather belt. Twice! He was a big dude. By God's miracle, I don't have a scar and didn't lose teeth. I was four."

Her thoughts come quickly and unguarded. It's as if she's told this story so many times, it no longer has power over her.

"I remember getting taken away from my biological family the first time when I was three. We, my older brother and I, now had a baby sister—around a year old at this time. We arrived at our foster home terrified, to say the least. But we quickly grew attached to our foster parents and their biological kids. That was ripped away from us a year later. I cried so hard. I screamed that I didn't want to leave. I begged them not to send me away. As the case worker's car drove down the drive, I twisted in my car seat, reaching my hand behind me, hoping that Mommy and Daddy would run after us, take us back, and allow us to stay. I remember seeing the tears of pain and heartbreak in the case worker's eyes as she looked in the rearview mirror and told me to stop twisting around. We were being taken from the people who loved us, who didn't neglect us or abuse us. From the one place we'd ever felt safe. They put us back into our nightmare we had wished to forget. When we arrived at the house where my biological mother lived, we found that we not only had a stepfather but a new little sister too—not his kid. Now, not only did we live with an abusive mother but also an abusive stepfather and his abusive family."

The abuse and neglect, and the shuttling back and forth between foster care and Amelia's mom, dragged on until the court finally terminated her mom's parental rights.

But Amelia stuns me with a glimpse of her heart for her birth mom. She's not vindictive.

"I still loved my mother, and I know deep down she loved me too. She was just too young to be a mother, and she didn't have the right and godly influences in her life to know how to take care of three very young children. Her mother, my grandmother, had a lot of medical problems. She also had substance abuse issues. Grandma may have drank when she was pregnant with Mom."

The three of us try to make sense of the past.

"I think the environment has something to do with it," Amelia says. "But she had choices to make. It is ultimately up to her choices." Her voice is mature and stable.

"What about mental illness?" I ask, thinking mental illness would introduce the idea of empathy and help the three of us understand the fuller truth.

Amelia nods. "Mental illness may be the reason, but it isn't an excuse to act out. She knows right from wrong. She should at least try. She still says our diagnoses are false and that the court lied. She blames me for us getting taken away because I wasn't watching the kids. I was five. I've talked to her. She still doesn't take responsibility for her decisions."

"Dang," I mutter quietly. "How does this make you feel about her?"

"I still love her, but I don't trust her. I've forgiven her, but I won't call her 'Mom.'"

Amelia knows that forgiveness doesn't always lead to reconciliation. Her mom isn't safe. She steers clear of this toxic relationship, as she should. Forgiveness like this is a hard choice for anyone who has experienced childhood trauma. But it has the potential to set a person free from the anger and hurt that has a hold on them.

Our booth is like a safe oasis, and our emotions are parched. We sip our ice waters and take a breather. I sit back and think. Given Amelia's story, the whole forgiveness thing makes me crazy inside my head. The only way I know how to forgive like this is to know how Jesus forgives, and trust his lead. Forgiving her mom was by far the last thing I expected Amelia to do, but she did. What would it be like if more of us learned to forgive like that?

"How old were you when you made a conscious decision to forgive your mom?" I ask.

"Eighteen."

Amelia says she learned about forgiveness and grace by watching her adoptive parents extend forgiveness and grace, over and over, to her and her siblings. Surrounded by farmland, cats, rabbits, and a house full of struggling siblings, Amelia's perception of God grew. Thanks to Saturday pizza night and Thursday dessert night with Crock-Pot chocolate lava cake, her perception of many things changed, one day at a time.

"The road to recovery isn't easy." Amelia says. "Don't be afraid to open up. It might seem scary at first, but it helps the recovery to happen faster once you do."

The leftover mile-high nachos get crammed and maneuvered into a white Styrofoam to-go container. Tori isn't sure they'll fit. I tend to agree. But Amelia makes it happen.

"You'll have nachos for dinner and a snack for the next two days!" I laugh.

> ## IT'S ONE THING TO HAVE BEEN HURT AND NEGLECTED BY YOUR FIRST PARENTS; IT'S ANOTHER THING TO SOMEHOW ARRIVE AT A PLACE OF LETTING GO OF THE HURT AND NEGLECT AND FORGIVE.

Days later, I'm still thinking about how Amelia forgave her mom. She's a forgiver, that one. It's one thing to have been hurt and neglected by your first parents; it's another thing to somehow arrive at a place of letting go of the hurt and neglect and forgive. Not forget but forgive. For Amelia, forgiveness was a step she took to take back control of her life again. Forgiveness can do that for you too.

Forgiveness—letting go of your right for resentment and revenge—may be something new for you to consider. The idea may even seem off the charts at first, even cringeworthy. But the more you ponder it, the more you will remember the times you've been forgiven. It starts to make sense. And in case you missed it, Amelia didn't forgive and forget. She won't be mistreated by her abuser again. She's set boundaries that keep her physically and emotionally safe. Ponder forgiveness; see if it makes sense for you.

CHAPTER 8

EMOTIONAL TUG-OF-WAR

As long as you keep secrets and suppress information,
you are fundamentally at war with yourself. . . .
The critical issue is allowing yourself to know what you know.
That takes an enormous amount of courage.

BESSEL VAN DER KOLK

LAST WINTER, I found myself at a Friday night high school basketball game, shoulder to shoulder with thousands of screaming fans. The floor-to-ceiling bleachers were packed. The game was close. The halftime buzzer sounded. The student section spilled out onto the shiny maple-plank court and collected into opposing teams. It was the halftime tug-of-war between the classes: freshmen against the sophomores first, then juniors against the seniors. Winners face off. Bragging rights were on the line. You know the scene, right?

Before the teams squared off along the thick, heavy braided rope, team captains carefully chose an anchor to fortify a strong footing for a better chance at winning. A good anchor can make all the difference. If you've ever played or watched tug-of-war, you know what's involved: two opposing sides on one heavy rope, pulling hard against each other until every muscle from the players' faces to their feet is engaged, straining and pulling and screaming until the winning team is called.

That night, in an unexpected twist, the lanky sophomores upset the seniors. The place went wild. Teammates climbed on top of each other like million-dollar lottery winners. No one would hear the end of it for days, maybe weeks. I thought, *What is it about the struggle that releases something deep within, something like grit and determination, just when you need it most?*

Have you ever been in a tug-of-war? Let me shift the question: Have you ever been in an emotional tug-of-war? Odds are, yes. It's pretty common. The thing is, most of us don't know how to summon our grit and determination to win this type of war on our own. We haven't assembled a team. We don't have a solid anchor to give us an edge. This I know: You can't win a tug-of-war by yourself. No one-person team can.

Cosette was seventeen, a junior in high school, when she experienced an ongoing emotional tug-of-war she remembers all too well—a battle between truths and lies. Lies like "You are not worthy or good enough." Lies that tug at your heart so hard they feel too real and impossible to ignore. Cosette says it was exhausting. The lies often won. And when the lies won, she felt defeated. Until she picked a solid anchor. That's when the tide turned. Having an anchor made all the difference.

Today Cosette is nineteen. She was born Guo Li Ping in Zhanjiang, a large, sprawling city in Guangdong Province of China. Two days after she was born, a local found her abandoned in plain sight and delivered her to the safety of an orphanage. Guo Li Ping was a sickly baby and failed to thrive at the orphanage. She had a rough start. She was brought to a foster family with a mom and dad and three foster siblings, where she was adored and slowly recovered. She met all the baby milestones—chubby legs, peekaboo, and all—without missing a beat. She was thriving.

At fourteen months, Guo Li Ping was adopted by a happy Texas couple in their midthirties, and she became a happy Texas toddler in her little Texas boots. She was showered with hugs and kisses, security, and plenty of love and attention. They named her Cosette, she says, after a little girl in the movie *Les Misérables* with a story similar to hers. She grew up watching PBS Kids. *Fetch! with Ruff Ruffman* and *Cyberchase* were her favorites. She wore tiaras and pink gowns. She snuggled in sleeping bags with girlfriends. She stirred the batter and licked the spoon helping her mom bake cookies for tea parties. She was a huggable, lovable little girl who was wanted and loved unconditionally.

All this goodness and love helped shape Cosette into the beautiful, active Texan she is today. After five years of competitive cheer, she's now a Dallas–Fort Worth college sophomore taking seventeen credits, studying social work, working weekends, and managing a long-distance relationship with her boyfriend. She admits she stress-bakes, and when she's in school she bakes a lot. She's also a foodie who loves the Dallas food scene but is always down for a bag of chips, Chick-fil-A, or, as she emphasizes, any kind of candy. Her goals are to graduate college and move on to adulthood. Important things stress her out. I say it's a good stress, and she's handling it beautifully.

But to end her story there would be leaving out an important piece. There's more that also shaped her, and it didn't begin in Texas. It began in China when she was born. There she experienced the two separations, losses that resurfaced in her junior year of high school.

Cosette tells me she was nervous to share her story. It's not easy sharing uncomfortable, messy feelings with the world. But she has stepped up because she has something she needs to say, things she couldn't make sense of when she was seventeen but can now.

She remembers it this way.

"I believed I was unlovable, unwanted, and unattractive. I had no other proof to counteract the lies. I was abandoned as an infant and figured my birth parents didn't want to keep me."

"These feelings would just come up?" I ask.

"Yes."

"What would happen?"

"Under the power of believing that I wasn't wanted, I became sad, timid, and shy. At times I would shut myself in my room after school and just cry in my bed. Sometimes I would go take a shower so that my parents didn't hear me cry. I would isolate myself, shutting everyone out. I would stop hanging out with friends and family and just want to stay by myself."

Cosette says she didn't know what to do. She says she couldn't share her feelings with her parents. As we sort through her thoughts and memories, she reveals she didn't want to make her mom and dad feel bad. Beyond that, she couldn't make sense of it.

She was having intense feelings of rejection. And with no one to blame, no one to help her voice her guilt and shame, she blamed herself. She thought being abandoned was all her fault. She thought she was bad or had done something wrong way back when she was an infant, and that's why she was given away. The shame and guilt would stay away during the day, while she was distracted with cheer and friends and school, but at night, when she was alone with her thoughts, the painful emotions would surface, to the point that they affected her outlook on life.

She wasn't the first. I had heard this from others too. Kids often blame themselves when things go wrong in their world. That's what Cosette did; she blamed herself.

"I was confused on why I felt this way," she says.

"What way?"

"I felt defective. I just felt empty and hurt. I felt lonely. I had friends, but I felt like I was alone in the world." She continues, "I shut people out of my life."

"Why?" I gently ask.

"That confuses me still. I don't know why."

"What did it look like to shut people out? Did you act out or push them away?"

"I've never acted out on my anger," she says. "If I was upset or struggling, sure, I'd get angry with my parents. Sometimes kids yell at their parents or do something that they aren't supposed to do. But I never once yelled at my parents. I never acted out. I think the worst I did was roll my eyes and get in trouble for that."

She pauses to think. "Growing up, I've always had the feeling and need to be perfect for my parents. I felt like if I wasn't perfect, they were going to abandon me."

She continues, "I also am not a person to talk about my feelings. Ever since we adopted my younger brother [not biologically related], I've always pushed down my feelings because I didn't want to add on to the stress of my parents."

Junior year turned into months of solitude, sadness, and isolation.

"What did that feel like?"

"I felt empty."

Her body was also responding, feeling weak, because that's what follows when self-doubt slips in.

"What did you do next?"

"I went to God," she confesses.

"You went to God?"

She says she could go to God before she went to her parents.

"It's always been my habit to seek God's Word when I'm struggling in something," she explains. "I don't talk about my feelings. I get closed off, so I usually deal with all of this internally."

"By yourself?"

"Yes."

"You were at your lowest point, by yourself, and you turned toward God?"

"I was desperate."

"What did you do?"

She thinks back. "I was in my room. I grabbed my Bible. I knew what God thought about me."

She crawled on her bed and found a verse that spoke into the emptiness she was experiencing.

"In John 15:16, it says, 'You did not choose me, but I chose you and appointed you so that you might go and bear fruit—fruit that will last—and so that whatever you ask in my name the Father will give you.'"

"So what were you scrambling for?"

"The truth. The more I read the truth, the more I believed it."

"A shift took place?"

"Yes. Slowly, God's truth overwhelmed the lies."

"So when you couldn't open your heart to your parents, you opened up to God?"

"Yes," she says. "I intentionally memorized encouragement

like this. I wanted to speak it over myself when I felt abandoned or unwanted."

"What happens in the moment when you speak God's Word into your fear and doubt, in moments when you feel defective and unworthy?" I ask.

"I feel a relief of fresh air. I feel the power of the Lord come over me. Most importantly, I feel warmth—it's like a dad welcoming his kid into his arms."

"You said this was your habit, to open up to God and listen for reassurance. Not once, but over and over and over again. Like learning a new cheerleading stunt, you have to practice to get better at hearing the truth."

"Yes, that is what I'm trying to do."

Cosette says she puts her trust in God because she knows the pull to believe she is unwanted is an ongoing battle. She needs help and she knows it.

"Do you believe lies such as 'You are unwanted' or 'You are defective' are common for adoptees?" I ask.

"I do believe that lies like these are pretty common. I think, being adopted, there are a lot of ways the devil can sneak in. The devil uses our insecurities and struggles and fear to plant seeds of doubt, especially to make me doubt what God says about me."

> **KNOWING SHE IS CREATED FOR A PURPOSE, SHE IS ENCOURAGED RATHER THAN BEING DEEPLY DISCOURAGED.**

"What does God say about you?"
"He says I am his creation. And he wants me!"

"Tell me more."

"He chose me to be his daughter. In Genesis 1:27, it says, 'God created mankind in his own image, in the image of God he created them; male and female he created them.'"

Knowing she is created for a purpose, she is encouraged rather than being deeply discouraged.

"I can sense God is your anchor in this emotional tug-of-war."

"Yes, God is my anchor," she says. "Honestly, I don't know where I would be without his presence in my life. Without God's Spirit living in me, speaking his truth, I think I would be lost and confused. I would feel abandoned."

Cosette confesses she still has moments of doubt. It's a journey. She knows shame and self-doubt can hold her back.

"To this day, it's still hard to remember that I was chosen."

She adds, "I still manage to struggle with this off and on, and I just go back to the Word of God and remember who he says I am. He says I am chosen."

Even so, she confesses there are some moments when the tug to believe she is unwanted is too hard to handle on her own.

"One of the things I'm realizing is that I need to talk about the way that I feel and not get closed off. Finding a community where I can talk about the struggles that I face would help."

I tell her to follow her instincts. It isn't my place, but I encourage her to get help. Ask, explore, open up, be vulnerable with her parents, her boyfriend, in a group or online community. Opening up is worth the risk. Other teens have told me this over and over. There must be something to it.

When you'd rather hide or let lies take hold and pull you down, do what Cosette did. Seek God's guidance and strength.

God is by far your best option for an anchor on your team. His truth is more powerful than the lies you will encounter. My hope for Cosette and you is that you will place God and a few trusted people on your team, so when the tug-of-war between truth and lies gets tough, you will have a team in place and an anchor that will increase your chances of winning the battle. After all, you can't win a tug-of-war on your own.

YOU'RE NOT ALONE

WE'VE BEEN THERE TOO

*What do you do with the mad
that you feel?*

MISTER ROGERS

CHAPTER 9

PERFECT MATCH

The things that make me different are the things that make me.

HARRY ARENDS

THIRTY-YEAR-OLD BEN HAS endless energy. He says it is how he was made. He's an endurance biker whose next race will take him 210 miles from Michigan's east coast to its west coast on gravel roads and sandy two-tracks.

He's excited because this time he will ride with five friends, each taking turns drafting off each other and leading the pack. Think the Tour de France peloton, sort of. But he's not in it to win. He says there's no way he will come in at the top ten. He competes against himself.

"You must be a machine," I say out of reverence.

He's humble and doesn't respond. Instead he says his five friends are very supportive of each other. "It's a lot of fun. First you feel great. After about six or seven hours, you don't feel so great. At the end, your whole body feels very heavy, like a weighted blanket is on it. You have no energy left to lift a cup after pushing the pedals that long."

Ben loves the idea of seeing how far he can go, even though he says it will take about a week to walk again. "It's a great feeling to post on Strava a better time than your friends."

He also loves a little thing called fly-fishing.

"I really wanted to try it," he offers. "I dove in pretty hard."

He took lessons and described casting in his backyard or at the park.

"It's kind of like golf; little changes can make a big difference. I'd go to the river and try. You know you're learning when you catch a fish."

He spent hours in the river braced in his waders against the current. While most guys were hanging out at a local coffee shop, he was hanging out at a local fly-fishing shop, bingeing on technique books and asking questions.

He laughs. "The guys there were cool. They saw I was hooked."

Eventually he became an instructor, taking customers to the river, teaching them how to cast, showing them different ways to fly-fish, and explaining all about flies when they were tired of casting. He's even written short stories about fly-fishing for specialty magazines.

"You sound like a high-energy, outdoorsman type of guy. So, where did this all come from?" I ask.

"Not my dad. He's not an outdoorsman. Neither is my mom or sister. I'm the only one. It's nature versus nurture. It's the biological part of who I am coming out."

I say, "You told me in an earlier conversation that as a teenager you wanted to be different than how you were made. That's obviously not how you feel today. In fact, it seems to me the way you were made is the key to your happiness. What were you like as a teen?"

He begins describing himself as a high-energy, active kid with low self-worth. I'm surprised. It doesn't match the guy I'm talking to.

"My adoptive dad and my mom lived in Hong Kong when they adopted my sister and me from the Philippines, a tropical country composed of seven thousand islands in Southeast Asia. To give you a simple picture of our family, us kids look Asian-Spanish, our mom is Heinz 57 American, and our dad is half Mexican and half American. We moved around a lot for my dad's business, and we traveled even more. My passport is full of stamps from thirty-eight countries."

"It sounds like an amazing upbringing, a bit unusual but highly exciting," I say.

"Yes. Unlike most kids, I grew up traveling the world, and that's why we are a close-knit family. We had our own strong family culture."

"I'm still a bit confused. What eroded your self-worth?" I ask.

"Every teenager is going to have insecurities or some insecurity about something. It is a rare teenager that doesn't. Sometimes it is the way you look or how people look at you. The teenager who doesn't have any insecurity is very lucky."

Ben's began when he was fourteen, when his family moved to London.

He describes living in the suburbs south of London, where traffic was lighter and there were more traditional houses compared to the city. While he and his sister went to school, Dad worked and Mom stayed busy volunteering. One day, he and his mom were at the grocery store going through the checkout lane. While she emptied the cart of bread and milk and veggies on the belt, he slipped behind his mom to the end of the belt and started bagging their groceries.

"That's when the cashier turned to me and shouted, 'Those aren't yours!'"

"What did you do?" I ask.

"I froze."

"So the cashier assumed you were stealing groceries?"

"Yes, but my mom quickly said, 'That's my son!'"

"On the way home, it hit me. People don't look at me and naturally think I am a part of my family. You know, white mom, brown kid," he says.

Dang, I thought to myself. He says it stung deep.

"I was getting to the age where I noticed for the first time that people would stare at my mom and me, trying to figure us out."

Ben describes how hard it was to look different from his parents.

"I loved my family so much, and I just wished I blended in."

Like most kids his age, he wanted to belong and wanted others to see that he belonged too.

"As a teenager, you don't want to be embarrassed," he says. "You just want to fit in."

My mom would say, "You were made in your birth mother's womb for us." But her words didn't change the fact that I still wanted to be different from how I was made.

"I wanted to look like them," he adds. In contrast, his sister was okay with her darker skin. He says everybody handles things differently.

Ben says the most sensitive time of his life was during high school in London. Feeling different made him question his worth. At times he felt he didn't have any worth, and he thought those feelings would last forever.

"I thought I would always be woeful. Man, was I blind. Thankfully, I also had a life and things I loved to do, so I wouldn't dwell on things too much."

Ben played drums in jazz band. He says that helped give him a purpose. Solo drum concerts also built his self-esteem.

"Somehow I can picture you jamming on the drums, knowing who you are today," I tell him.

He also played soccer and rugby too. It felt great to help his team. And somewhere between kicking the ball and kicking himself for looking different, he grew up.

"I gave my parents plenty of reason not to love me at times."

"You don't seem the type," I say.

"You know we do that when we are teens, right?" We laugh, both guilty of it. "But my parents were always loving and encouraging, even when I was super angsty or mad. They gave me the space I needed. They really cared, and eventually I noticed."

"So you're saying you struggled with looking different from your family. But over time, you learned not to be defined by your skin color or how you look?"

"What I was feeling as a teen was valid. When you're in that moment of life, questioning, wanting life to be different, things seem magnified."

Looking back, Ben noticed there was a lot of love from his mom and dad encouraging him through that tough season.

I wonder if other teens with similar thoughts notice as much as Ben did.

"God gave me the parents I have. I love them beyond words. And yes, it took me a long time to give that feeling of being different up to God. But I did. I remember talking to God and realizing he was not going to change the way I look, and he made me this way for a reason. I wish I knew that as a teen. If someone would have told me that, I would have viewed my skin color and race differently and been encouraged by it." He goes on, "Your family doesn't care what you look like; they care about what you believe and what you care about and how you are on the inside. Acceptance goes deeper than how you look. I love my family. If God were going to make an adoptive family, he made mine a perfect match for me. When it comes to personality, I am like my mom, and my sister is more like my dad."

"So you're a mix of nature versus nurture, like you said earlier?"

"Yes."

I ponder his answer. "So you are saying nobody gets to be Ben Gandy but you?"

> **YOU ARE MADE IN GOD'S IMAGE JUST THE WAY YOU ARE SUPPOSED TO BE. . . . NOBODY ELSE GETS TO BE YOU BUT YOU.**

"That's right," he says.

"You are made in God's image," Ben continues, "just the way you are supposed to be. That is the advantage you have. Nobody else gets to be you but you. You get to represent God like nobody else and in your own unique way. The way you live out your life can teach others about God in a way only you can do."

CHAPTER 10

FULL CIRCLE

Weeping is perhaps the most human and most universal of all relief measures.

KARL MENNINGER

WHEN AMBER WAS a teenager she joined the high school track team and ran hurdles and high jump. It sounds simple, even typical, but for Amber, who was adopted at birth, it was so much more.

"For me, jumping hurdles was a way to share something in common with my birth mom. We had a closed adoption. I knew some things, but I couldn't look for her until I was eighteen, so I chose track because she did it."

Amber had scanned her adoption paperwork for ideas and took up one of her birth mother's interests as a way to stay connected to her. She says she needed that connection until she could search for her birth mother. Open adoptions weren't as common then, so in a way, it was her best effort to keep her mother's memory alive.

"I tried to find a way to honor her just like you would honor someone who is deceased."

Who knew that jumping hurdles would be both a physical and emotional sport?

Amber, now in her early thirties, was domestically adopted and raised in a small town near the shores of Lake Michigan with her mom and dad and older brother. In high school she was a competitive athlete, a certified band geek who played in the percussion section, and, she admits, a terrible student. She didn't see the point. She had a brain; she just didn't have a vision for her future. Not uncommon at seventeen. But after her cap and gown were stored away and her running shoes were lost who knows where, she worked a little, cleared her head, and became a college student. She graduated as a paralegal in two years and met her future husband around the same time. Today she's no longer a paralegal because she and her husband adopted their first child, baby Liam.

"My story isn't fancy," she tells me from her living room over the phone. "I knew plenty of adopted kids growing up, and we didn't have tragic stories. It's always been a part of my life. It's not different to me to be adopted."

Still, Amber was, like most adopted kids, curious. She remembers being in middle school when her curiosity caught up with her. She had all the usual questions. What did her birth mother look like? Would she ever get to meet her?

"My parents reassured me many, many times that her decision to make an adoption plan was *not* easy and that it was made out of love. This took me time to process; it took time to accept. I put myself in her shoes. How hard would that have been? Would I have been able to do that? Definitely not! I had a lot of respect for her because of that. She chose to give me what she couldn't: two parents, an older brother, a stable home, and probably many other things I can't think of now. It was a loving decision. Still, I really struggled with accepting that I may never meet my birth mom."

At this point, Amber and I have been on the phone for over an hour. She says I can ask her anything. So I do.

"What did struggling look like for you?"

"I was around twelve and was starting to grasp the big picture of what adoption is. One night I had a random breakdown at my church youth group. Out of nowhere it hit me. Some lady was singing a song. I couldn't tell you what song it was or even who sang it. Kids in my circle and my youth group leader were asking me, 'What's wrong, what's wrong?' I am one of those people who, if I'm on the verge of tears, if you hug me it will make it worse."

"What was going on?"

"I remember crying."

"Do you recall why you cried?"

"I missed my birth mother. But how could I miss someone I had never met? This was silly. It wasn't logical."

"You had to start somewhere, right, working through your loss?" I offer.

"I don't know how to explain it. It felt like the death of a loved one. I think the full weight of the situation hit me. I do tend to be the type of person that holds things in, and then it all just spills out."

"Did you ever lose anyone before this?"

SAD IS AN HONEST EMOTION.

"My grandpa died when I was in second grade. That was the first time really dealing with a loss."

"Sad is an honest emotion," I point out.

"Yes, but crying felt kind of stupid because I didn't know the person I was crying over. At that point in my life, I thought I may never meet her. So there was nothing I could do about it but grieve her. My parents talked with me and I felt better. After that, I never really had any major emotional breakdowns. After that time in middle school when I broke down, I was okay. I got it. Like my story finally sunk in."

Years later, at twenty-two, Amber got married. She worked at a law firm, and her husband worked in heating and cooling. But from time to time, she'd get curious. At one point, she decided to look for her birth mother. One night she got lucky and thought she found her on Facebook. Actually, she says her husband did. But she wasn't certain it was her mom. Not wanting to get her hopes up in case it wasn't, she searched online for a "first letter for contacting your birth mother" template. She made some edits, copied and pasted some words, and messaged the woman they found on Facebook. To her surprise, the woman responded the next day. Amber was amazed!

"Then what happened?"

"Lots of tears."

"I can't put myself in your shoes, so what kind of tears?"

"Relief. Joy. Shock. All of the above. Mostly happy. Feeling a whole lot of things at once. It was incredibly emotional. We chatted online for a while. I even learned that I had a younger half brother. Eventually, we met at a parade. Lots of crying. Happy tears. Awkwardness, like a first date in a way. At least for me. Weird small talk trying to make a connection. We hugged. It was happy-awkward. We slowly warmed up. The weirdest part about it was seeing someone else who actually looked like me. I *actually* looked like someone else. It was so obvious. The chin, mouth, and nose . . . all three of us—birth mom, half brother, and myself—had the same ones. I still look at the one picture we took together and think how crazy that is to me, when looking like your family is so normal for almost everyone else.

"That's the only time I met her."

"Just once? I'm surprised. Was that all you needed?"

"Yes. I just wanted to hug her at least once and let her know I turned out okay. It was all I needed. I wasn't looking for a relationship. I also wanted her to know I didn't resent her for her decision. We talk on Facebook from time to time. I told her she can reach out to me whenever she wants to. She hasn't. She left the ball in my court, and I think she may not want to overstep boundaries."

"So how did it help you, meeting your birth mother and all, even if only once?"

"I really just wanted to know what she looked like. That was the biggest lingering question I had."

A few years later Amber and her husband adopted a newborn baby boy. She was blessed to have a front-row seat to what her birth mother experienced years back when she carefully handed Amber to another family to raise.

"Though heartbreaking to watch, seeing my son's birth mom hold him before leaving the hospital was the most beautiful display of love I have ever seen. I watched as this teenage young woman held her son for the first time; not saying anything, just letting the tears fall and land on this tiny baby boy swaddled up in a hospital blanket. I sat on the floor next to her, letting her have as much time as she needed. How could I not? She was giving my husband and me the most precious gift in the world. I was going to get to hold him every day and she wasn't. All she had was her trust in us to keep in touch with her, and trust that we were going to let her see him again. It was one of the most beautiful love scenes I've ever seen. I'm thankful for her trust. It's been three years. She and I text several times a week, and we see her and her family a few times a year. I'm happy that my son won't have the same questions I had growing up. He will know her name, how old she is, and what she looks like and more. And maybe he will grieve someday, but in his own way."

Amber acknowledges that some adopted kids will never meet their birth mother. Still, she knows firsthand: "She loves you! It was probably the toughest decision she ever had to make.

"I always knew my birth mother made her decision out of love. Seeing Liam and his birth mom together, and her handing him to me, it came full circle."

I hear Liam's little voice in the background. Amber explains he's trying to ride on the back of their five-month-old Australian shepherd. We both laugh and wander off topic to talk about dogs for a while.

And all those years of not knowing in middle school and high school? Amber says it's okay to feel loss and grieve in a healthy way. We all have our own unique way of handling loss. Work through your emotions the best way you can and in your own way, no matter how sloppy and teary-eyed you get. You will heal your heart and become stronger if you do.

CHAPTER 11

ON BEING HEARD

Practicing mindfulness, emotional awareness, and supportive self-talk helps. Rarely do we heal by accident. We must actively participate in our own getting well.

JENNIFER HEALEY

RAYNE WAS NINETEEN when she worked part-time as an eyewear consultant at LensCrafters in Tampa. It was a great job for a college student to make some gas money and help pay for school expenses. Her main job? Pointing clients to frames that fit their look, such as Ralph Lauren, Ray-Ban, and Vogue eyeglasses. In a way, Rayne was an eyewear fashion consultant—no experience necessary. She had a good eye for fashion and could handle the details, such as helping clients pick from a menu of lens options so they could see with crystal clarity. That's the irony of her story, she says: she works with people to help them see, yet some are so blind to the feelings of others.

Today, Rayne is twenty-three, a student heading into a master's program in forensics. She describes herself as vibrant and loud, with a wink of sarcasm and a quick sense of humor. But there's more. She has strong convictions and gets incredibly passionate about helping people who are disadvantaged. Empathy oozes from her, perhaps hardwired like that from infancy.

Music is her love. She composes music and plays her violin to relax. As far as family life, she's big into pasta and spending time with her friends and her loud, lovable Cuban-Italian family that she'd never trade for the world.

Flashback to 1997. As a newborn, Rayne was abandoned on the steps of a police station in hot and muggy Nanjing, Jiangsu, China, and brought to the Gaoyou City Children's Welfare Institute. Twelve months later, she was adopted by a Cuban-Italian couple, originally from New York and now living in Tampa, Florida. She tells me the rest is a blank page.

"There are some adoptees who know their birth parents or maybe know some family history. Not me. I don't have the slightest clue who my parents are or who my biological family is. I don't even know when my real birthday is; it's just an approximation."

Rayne confesses that the "not knowing" bothers her from time to time. It mostly ramps up when she gets intrusive, insensitive questions from strangers, which was common while growing up.

"Most of my life, there have been these small, seemingly insignificant moments that would prompt a little voice in my head to remind me, *Hey! You're not part of your family. You're adopted.* I mean, I've always known I was adopted. It was never something that my family hid from me—which would be kind of hard since I'm Chinese and my family is Italian-Cuban.

"Being asked about my 'origin story' never bothered me. In fact, I enjoyed sharing it. Maybe it is a little cynical, but I loved seeing the look on people's faces, as if they were thinking, 'Wow! I don't know what I would do if I didn't know my birthday,' and so on. In a way, I like knowing that they wonder what it would be like for them to not know who their biological family is; to have them, for only a moment, wonder what it is like to lose your identity."

As Rayne describes all this, she also admits most people—strangers and new acquaintances included—question her out of pure, innocent curiosity. In other words, she doesn't normally mind. Still, there will always be questions that are intrusive and, in a word, ignorant. One of her worst experiences was at LensCrafters one afternoon, while fitting a customer for glasses.

"Working in retail, I learned that making a personal connection was something clients enjoyed, so sharing that I am adopted came up often," she explains.

"And that was okay?" I ask curiously.

"Yes, except for the time a middle-aged gentleman and his wife came in to pick up his new glasses." She continues. "He started talking to me about his family. Then he asked where my family was from. I perked up with a smile and said New York. Next he asked me where they are *from* from."

"*From* from?"

"Yeah, *from* from. I told him my family is Italian and Cuban. He chuckled and then blurted, 'How did *that* happen?' I casually told him that I'm adopted. He chuckled some more, leaned forward in his chair to try on his new glasses, and said, 'So you mean your real parents didn't want you?'"

My jaw drops. "Seriously? Who says that?"

"Yes, seriously. His wife, who was sitting next to him, let out a muffled laugh. The exchange happened so fast that all I said back was, 'Yeah. I guess so!' and laughed along with them."

"Okay, can I say some people are dumb?" Now I'm feeling defensive for my newfound friend.

"I know, right?"

She goes on to explain that after her ten-hour shift, after clocking out, she walked to her Honda CR-V as the sun was setting, slid in, and grabbed the wheel—like, *really* grabbed it, with all her might. That's when something clicked. The man's words had triggered something.

"Sitting there, I thought about his question, his laugh, his wife joining in. I thought about what I said back and how I brushed it casually aside," she says. "As I gripped the wheel harder, my heart began pounding, my face got hot, and I felt anxious. I wanted to scream. I wanted to curse. I wanted to punch something."

"You were angry!" We are entering a sensitive space, and I tread carefully.

"I was filled with anger, but not toward them. Toward me."

"Wait, why you?"

"A little voice came back, taunting me: *Hey! You're not part of your family. You're adopted.* I was angry that I had accepted what that man said as truth: *My real parents didn't want me.*"

I rub my forehead between my eyes. "So you're saying you accepted the lie even though you know the truth? Can you explain why this happened? You seem grounded and strong and emotionally levelheaded. What happened back then?"

"It's a difficult, conflicting feeling when it comes to believing someone's words when you know, logically, they aren't true," Rayne answers.

"So it wasn't a rational reaction?" I ask.

"Yes," she agrees. "I was extremely emotional at the

time—angry, frustrated, sad—and since I've struggled with my identity all my life and have constantly had to reassure myself of who I am, it was just a moment of weakness where all of that growth seemed to be thrown by the wayside, even for a moment."

I think about what she says. How this man's rude comment triggered the trauma she holds close.

"I admire how you can look back and see what was going on and make sense of it now. Tell me what happened after that breakdown in your car?"

"For a while after this happened, I dipped into a major identity crisis."

"Nooo." I groan. "What happened?"

"I had always told myself that I am a Chinese-Italian American and that I was proud of it. But now I thought to myself that I didn't belong to any of those. Having no Chinese influence, I had no right to consider myself Chinese. Being Chinese, I had no right to consider myself Italian. Not being born in America, I had no right to consider myself American. For a time, I felt so lost and alone. Lots of confusion welled up."

"I think I understand," I say, unable to relate. "I'm not sure how best to phrase this, but it sounds like there was a wounded little girl from the past inside you who needed reassurance?"

"Yes, there was. It was a version of myself from the period of time where I had begun to realize through social interactions in school that I was being rejected by the Asian community—being reminded by other Asian friends that I do not have Asian parents, Asian traditions, even authentic Asian food for lunch—and being rejected by other white Americans, who would stereotype me when I did not perform well on an exam, saying, 'You're supposed to be the Asian one,' to indicate I wasn't smart enough.

Throughout all those struggles, hearing this man say that my real parents didn't want me just attacked the child in me who didn't know who I was and reinforced the idea that I didn't belong anywhere. Especially because I have worked so hard on a personal level to accept who I am."

Rayne brings breath and voice to years of frustration and experiences that had taken their toll on her.

"Was it difficult to express your hurt and confusion to your parents or a close friend?" I ask.

"I wanted to talk to someone about what had happened and everything that I was feeling," she says, "but I felt like I couldn't because no one else could relate. I especially felt like I could not confide in my parents. I was afraid they would interpret my feelings as me rejecting them as my family and wishing I was not adopted because I felt like I didn't belong, and because it makes me wonder about my birth family. Looking back, I wish I had taken a chance to talk with someone."

I wish she had too, I think. Isolated thoughts can take on a life of their own.

Eventually, Rayne says, she found China's Children International (CCI), a Facebook group where hundreds of adoptees share their experiences and their stories. She opened up to them.

"I really didn't do any specific searching for anyone to talk to after the incident happened. It might have been about a year or two later, when I was twenty or twenty-one. I don't quite remember how it happened, to be honest, but I do know I got curious about my birth family again and was feeling insecure again, and I think I just did a random Chinese adoptee search on Facebook and found the group.

"I scrolled through the pages for hours, reading all the posts and comments of other adoptees having a feeling of not belonging anywhere, and this is where I finally felt like someone understood."

"All those kindred spirits," I smile. "That had to feel good."

"Knowing I wasn't alone in my thoughts, feelings, and experiences was relieving," she says. "It was the first time I felt like I finally belonged somewhere and was heard and understood. They were free to express how the loss of their birth parents has impacted their lives. I've befriended fellow adoptees! We share our insecurities and encounters with racism and ignorance. For the first time in my life, I felt heard."

"And being heard is everything?"

"Yes, and I also didn't feel like I had to defend anything, or feel awkward admitting I felt hurt and lonely."

"Yeah. You could be vulnerable, safe, no one to talk you out of your emotions," I add. "Just eager hearts ready to say, 'It's okay' and 'me too.'"

"It was a feeling of comfort and safety, like how it feels to curl up on the couch, wrap up in a warm Sherpa blanket, and sip a cup of hot cocoa at the end of the night."

I smile. "I like that image."

Rayne confesses she still has twinges from deep within where she feels insecure, and tiny nudges that test her resolve. Thanks to the group and her new acquaintances, though, she says the twinges and nudges come less and less.

"I have comfort knowing that there are others out there like me. I am not alone."

Rayne is proof that adoptees are resilient. Finding a community helped. She wants all teens reading her story to know this: You are not alone. We share a common ground and shared experiences.

China's Children International is a private Facebook group, so I don't have a link to share. However, if you are interested in joining the community, you can search for China's Children International on Facebook and it will show up.

> **SPEAKING ABOUT THE HURT, SAYING IT OUT LOUD, FINDING THE WORDS AND THE BRAVERY, NO MATTER HOW RAW AND AWKWARD, IS A RISK WORTH TAKING.**

I don't remember saying this to Rayne, but I realize, after spending so much time with young people who were adopted, that speaking about the hurt, saying it out loud, finding the words and the bravery, no matter how raw and awkward, is a risk worth taking. In other words, confronting the uncomfortable often leads us to a new level of comfort.

If finding kindred spirits is your next step, you can follow Rayne's lead. Or find or form a small group in your community or high school or college. That's how a group formed on campus at Michigan State University (see the Somewhere In Between Club appendix for their collective advice). They found each other and formed a bond. Together they share their stories, fears, hurts, wins, daily life, encouragement, and great food. Whether you find such a group in your community, online, or at your college campus, at least seek a kindred spirit to open up to that can relate. This must be why God says, "Two are better than one. . . . If either of them falls down, one can help the other up" (Ecclesiastes 4:9–10).

CHAPTER 12

A LIFE OF PURPOSE

One of the most important things you can do on this earth
is to let people know they are not alone.

SHANNON L. ALDER

STANDING IN FRONT of two hundred people was the last thing
Maria ever thought she'd do. Growing up, public speaking sent
shivers down her spine. But there, staring back at her, were teens
just like her—born in Guatemala and adopted by Americans—
and she needed to speak to them.

Her goal that day was to bring relief, understanding, and
peace, and help these kids understand who they are. "Funny,"
she says, "I was the least likely person to bring them hope. My
teen years were not very hopeful, and yet here I was ready to
bring it, a girl who had struggled with anxiety and fear and was
too ashamed to express it while growing up."

Maria was born in Coban Alta Verapaz, Guatemala, and
adopted by Americans at nine months old. Her parents took one
look at her and named her Maria "because they thought it was
both Spanish and American, so it fit." She grew up in Buffalo,
New York, where her dad taught her how to fish at age three. She
says autumn is her favorite time of year because it's not too hot
and not too cold, and it is that much closer to her three favorite

holidays, Halloween, Thanksgiving, and Christmas. Maria went to college in Buffalo, but currently lives in Pittsburgh in an apartment in South Park. She's thirty now and engaged to be married soon. And since 1993, her dad has been her favorite fishing buddy.

When I caught up with Maria, she was planning her next speaking event. She's a speaker who encourages and inspires adopted kids from Guatemala who grew up wondering why their birth parents couldn't keep them and who are trying to make sense of it all like her. She never visualized herself as a speaker while growing up, but it's now her passion. She also offers one-on-one online mentoring for other Guatemalan adoptees. We talked over the phone several times about her life as a teen and some advice she has to help teens struggling to find themselves.

"I was a short, four-foot-nine, awkward turtle-teen with braces," she says.

In contrast, her sister was perfect with blonde hair and stunning blue eyes.

"She was beautiful and I was not. At least, that's what I thought as a teen because I wasn't *that kind* of beautiful."

And even when she was told she was beautiful, "I couldn't believe it," she says.

In her mind, the difference between her sister and her was too glaring. Feeling awkward made it hard for her to fit in at school too. She says she felt different, so she shrank back and didn't want to go out. Staying home felt safer somehow. Like a self-quarantine.

"Home was my safe zone with my mom and dad. I didn't feel judged there like I did in school," she says. "Looking back, how I looked played a big role in the way I felt about myself and the decisions I made. And it generated a whole lot of anxiety."

It wasn't until her sophomore year that things began to settle down for Maria, but anxiety and low self-esteem still messed with her. She began trusting the world again only after she met two African American girls who befriended her and didn't judge her. They became her best friends.

"My friends helped me to break away from my safe zone. Why I thought everyone was judging me seems odd today."

"I think that's a teen thing. Maybe more so for adopted teens," I say.

She says low self-esteem is crippling, and it impacts everything. A life of anxiety is not what she wants for herself or others like her. Having struggled as a teen, as an adult she began encouraging adopted teens, first online and eventually onstage. She wants more for them. She often confesses from the stage how she felt as a teen:

- I didn't want to tell my mom stuff.
- I didn't want to sound hateful.
- I was too ashamed to express my feelings.
- My feelings were too hard for me to put into words.
- I didn't know who I was supposed to be. Am I supposed to be Hispanic?

Then she lays out her own brand of encouragement, the opposite of how she responded as a teen—kind of a "what not to do" list mixed with "what to do":

- You are not the weird kid. Don't go there.
- It is possible to feel conflicted emotions about your roots and your place in your family. It's normal and okay.

- Don't shut down. Reaching out is the best thing you can do.
- You can be real with your parents. They want that.
- You can express your fears and anxiety. You are stronger than you think.
- How you feel isn't crazy, no matter how raw and painful it is.
- Decisions you've made don't have to be forever. Rethink your decisions often.
- Find a mentor or group, people you have a common bond with, who really understand.
- Figure out how to be Guatemalan, because it is good and okay.
- Believe that you have a purpose. You do!
- Don't be like other people. Just be you.
- You are beautiful! You are!
- You are not alone!

While I haven't been to one of Maria's events, I can imagine her voice from the stage, bigger than her four-foot-nine frame, sending forth encouragement to a room full of teens nodding, "Me too."

"I'm like a big sister," she says. "We have a lot in common. They look to me for guidance, and because I'm Guatemalan and an adult, I can help them cope because I went through a lot of what they are going through. They can ask me anything—like, 'What did you do in this situation when you were my age?'"

"You're like a dream big sister," I say.

"I think it is my voice," she says. "Maybe these kids don't have the words to say the things they want to say or how they feel, but when I speak, it is exactly how they feel. When I describe how I felt as a teen, it's my voice for them."

"So you are giving them the words to use?" I ask.

"Yes. Now they know what to say to their moms and dads and they can express themselves."

"They can relate to you."

"Yes, and I can relate to them."

"That list you shared. You're asking teens to try like you did. That's risky for some, but it's a risk worth taking."

"I feel like these people are my family. I'm a voice of reassurance. These kids and I, we share more than our heritage—we share everything."

ONE DAY YOU'LL BE READY TO USE YOUR VOICE TO ENCOURAGE OTHERS. MAYBE IT'S NOW.

Who reassures you? Do you reassure others? Maybe you're not ready, but consider this: how you move through the ups and downs of life matters. One day you'll be ready to use your voice to encourage others. Maybe it's now.

Maria Wisniewski hosts an annual conference in Pittsburgh for Guatemalan adoptees and their families. Check out her Facebook group at https://www.facebook.com/groups/22630662 40419405/?ref=share.

CHAPTER 13

INSECURE TO SELF-ASSURED

Happiness and confidence are the prettiest things you can wear.

TAYLOR SWIFT

BEFORE BEAUTY FILTERS were even a thing, Emma took pictures of her face and wouldn't stop until she could whisper, "Perfect." Then she'd share, but only the perfect ones. It sometimes took ten to fifteen different poses, checking the angle, her nose, her lips, her hair; comparing and never feeling satisfied with the way she looked. What she didn't know at the time was that a nasty thing called insecurity was wrapping its grimy grip around her tender heart and trying to squeeze the life and joy and Emma out of her.

It's just past five on a Tuesday evening in October at Panera. The lines are short for now, the cinnamon-colored tables slowly filling with the early dinner crowd. I sit alone, having arrived ahead of Emma, a newly minted ESL teacher who works at an elementary school thirty minutes away. The aroma of freshly baked baguettes draws me to the menu on the back wall behind the counter. Then I spot Emma. She waves, still dressed in her floral-print Francesca's dress, a feminine confection that drapes elegantly over her five-foot-six, size-zero frame. We join each other at the counter to order. Since February, we've known each other through email, phone calls, and meeting up like this.

At twenty-four, Emma doesn't appear the least bit insecure. But when we sit down, she begins to explain her previous descent into insecurity as an Asian American teen.

"My insecurities were connected with my Asian features," she says. "It was so easy to compare myself to others and be sad. If I was seventeen again, in my bathroom with my phone taking picture after picture after picture, I wouldn't go through it again."

What had Emma gone through?

Emma was adopted from Jianxi, China, when she was nine months old. "I was a small baby and had a big belly," she explains. "I was very sick. In China, the orphanages have dying rooms for babies like me. The only reason I lived is that they knew I was being adopted and they gave me medicine. Thousands of babies die each year in dying rooms. You can watch documentaries about this," she says with a heavy heart.

My first thought is, *I can't. I won't.* Then with a heavy heart I reluctantly put it on my list to check it out later.

"Tell me about you," I say. "Who is Emma?"

"I have an old spirit," she explains. "I should have been born in the 1940s. I love letters over texts. I love slowness and baking like our grandmas did. I love the dress and style of the era."

We wonder together about this old soul that lingers and agree it has Asian roots. The space we share at the little table fills with quiet; then she tells me she believes her Asian roots play a big role in who she is. She longs to know more about her birth family, like so many do, but she says she is content not knowing.

"There is a sense of longing, but I know when I meet the Lord

I will know. The big questions will be answered then," she says with a smile. "I feel at peace. I have a social life, a fiancé, I am getting married soon. In this season of life, I feel established and content."

She's also a romantic. She modestly lifts her left hand and offers me a look at her silver and diamond engagement ring, all while telling me about her magical first kiss with the man of her dreams under a delicate snowfall. We lazily stay on this topic because I'm a romantic too.

"What's your love language?" I ask, curious how she feels loved.

"Quality time," she smiles. "Just being with family and friends makes me feel loved."

No wonder. She says she grew up in an idyllic home with lots of love, support, and care from her single mom, who single-handedly raised Emma and her younger sister, who is not biologically related. The sisters grew up going to church, learning about loving God and loving others. While she says she always felt cherished, Emma didn't always cherish the way she looked—like in third grade, when she wished she had smaller lips.

"In third grade, I started noticing I didn't look like my mom and that I am Asian. It was confusing. *Not only do I have a different family tree but I look different too*, I thought. That's when I wished I had smaller lips. I just didn't like them. I thought they were bigger than the rest of my face." She laughs now, but back then it was a big deal to a little girl.

"But you have beautiful, full lips," I truthfully say. Apparently I'm not the first to tell her so. She smiles. A memory surfaces of her aunt sitting crisscross applesauce on the living room floor, comforting her about her lips. Emma's tiny face is leaning into the blush brush as her aunt lightly applies pink blush to her cheeks, then finishes with a slight touch of pinkish red lip gloss on her lips. "Celebrities pay thousands of dollars to have lips like yours," her aunt tells her.

"It meant so much to me that she tried to help me. But it didn't change things right then and there."

"You wanted to fit in?" I ask.

"Yeah. I wanted thin lips because that's what Americans have. But eventually, I grew into my lips."

She adds, "My insecurity was short-lived. Third grade was not all about lips. It wasn't a hard time. It was just a confusing time."

Later on in high school, Emma's insecurities ramped up. This time she was insecure about her eyes. She explains how she wanted double eyelids instead of Chinese monolids. She fills me in on what this means while pointing to the wished-for missing crease.

"Sophomore year of high school, I got my own bathroom. I remember taking a selfie with my phone. Staring into the camera, I didn't like how my eyes looked."

"Did you practice trying to get the perfect look?" I ask.

"Yes!" Emma says. "I scrunched my forehead like this"—she demonstrates by lifting her brows—"and I liked how my eyes looked."

"Do it again, the scrunching thing," I say, watching her lift her brows, then trying the forehead maneuver myself.

"Lifting my brows makes my monolid look bigger and even like a double lid," Emma explains.

Looking closer, I watch her demonstrate the before and after again.

"See?" She scrunches her forehead. "You can see it resembles a double eyelid."

I look closely because I've never examined monolids before, and she laughs because she's never shown anyone her scrunching nor told anyone she scrunched. We both break out laughing hysterically at how funny we look scrunching in the middle of Panera.

But there's a downside to all this scrunching.

"I started noticing very mild wrinkles on my forehead even without scrunching," Emma says.

I lean in to look. Little lines have indeed formed on her forehead.

"I also felt bad when I had to scrunch my forehead to feel beautiful. It sounds so ridiculous to say it out loud. After a while, I didn't know how I looked without my forehead scrunched."

Truth is, Emma felt uncomfortable and didn't feel like she fit in a world of Caucasian eyes. The differences were upsetting.

Scrunching continued into college, and her insecurities grew. Sophomore year, while attending Grace College in Indiana, Emma learned about double eyelid surgery, a type of plastic surgery that creates creases in the upper eyelid to make the eye appear bigger. For some, the surgery is to create a "Westernized" eyelid.

"No! You weren't really thinking about eyelid surgery?" I ask, with a little worry in my voice.

"Yes," Emma says. "Some Asian women do this to accentuate this feature."

"I didn't know," I say. Wow. This was getting big.

"Yeah. My insecurity about how I looked became so extreme I wanted to take it to the next level."

I shake my head. "I have no idea what it feels like to live in a culture surrounded by people I don't look like."

"But I do," Emma replies. "If you grew up in a country of Asian women, your perception of beauty would be in conflict too."

She's right. "What happened next?" I ask.

"I started praying to God, 'Help me see myself the way you see me.' I knew in my heart the Lord saw me as beautiful. He created me. If it is God's truth that I am beautiful, then I needed to find my true beauty."

Despite her prayers, she was blinded by her insecurities. She was so focused on her looks that it made the lies she told herself easier to believe than the truth. "We can say nasty things to ourselves, like our eyes are too small or our lips too big, when we need to speak kindly into our hearts."

But while some people let their insecurities derail them, Emma did not. She says she loved high school; she was a runner, athlete, and leader, and she was successful in college.

"I still went through life," Emma says. "I still went out. I didn't hide in a corner. There were just lingering emotions."

Following college, after Emma accepted her first teaching job and had a consistent paycheck, she took a surprising next step. Surprising to her? No. To her family? Yes. She went for a consultation to have double eyelid surgery.

"So you were fresh out of college, new job and all? You still thought surgery was the solution?"

"Yes. The cost was steep, and I knew it was going to be financially tight, but I was willing to spend a couple thousand dollars to make it happen. Insecurity is extreme when you take it to the next level. It's one thing to wish for a solution; it's another thing to seek one. You need to ask yourself, is there a heart issue?"

"Did you?"

Emma shakes her head. "Not at first."

She made the call to schedule a consultation. That's when her family began speaking up.

"My mom loved me and told me she wouldn't be angry if I did it, but she told me she didn't like the idea of me messing with my eyes."

Her sister opened up too, in a very blunt and honest way.

"She told me, 'Your students will wonder why you are choosing to change your appearance to look more white. What will they think? Many of your students are Asian. Will they think they aren't as beautiful too, if you do that? What will you say?' Erica told the hard truth. Something not many people are willing to do."

Emma's boyfriend (now fiancé) supported her too, and even took a second job at the mall to help her pay for the surgery.

"What was he thinking?" I ask.

"I don't know," Emma says. "I didn't think he would get a second job. He wasn't even my husband, just my boyfriend at the time. It meant a lot. I think he thought I was serious. He thought there was nothing he could say or do that would change my mind. I didn't think I was letting anyone change my mind at the time."

That day in the doctor's office, the exam chair was cold and stiff, and the paper crinkled when Emma sat down. The consultation went quickly. A date was set. She had the money. She was convinced the surgery would be life-changing. She felt confident at the time. But would she have the heart to go through with it?

Not long after, something shifted. Unexpectedly. She says God showed her something new, something she couldn't see while blinded by her insecurities. He reminded her she already had a wonderful life—a wonderful family, a wonderful fiancé, her own apartment, a career, and so much more. While she was feeling insecure about her Asian features for so many years, wanting something she thought would relieve the pressure of fitting in, she had built a wonderful, secure life. She already fit in. She also realized she didn't want to crash her bank account when she could spend her money for her upcoming wedding.

"Am I truly content without the double eyelid surgery?" Emma says. "Since then, I never thought twice about it again. I still can't explain it. Sometimes the Lord works in your life and you don't even know it."

Emma senses God was working through her mom's love, her fiancé's support, and her sister's honesty. He was working through the people who loved her. She explained that there is nothing greater than experiencing the grace and love of God in the most tangible, concrete, and life-altering way.

> **THE ROOT OF DISCONTENTMENT IS WHEN YOU COMPARE YOURSELF TO ANYTHING.**

"I found contentment in how Christ sees me. I know that God created me like this and that I should not try to change how he made me."

Emma explains, "The root of discontentment is when you compare yourself to anything. I compared myself to Caucasians. When you compare yourself to anyone, you will always be dissatisfied. The same goes for teens when they apply beauty filters on their phones to look perfect. Contouring cheeks, tweaking your nose, changing the color of your hair . . . when taken too far, it points to insecurity."

She continues, "We all feel insecure at times. Don't take it to the next level. You'll never be content. If you are dealing with insecurities about your identity and race, talk to someone. Give it to the Lord. Process it with him. Insecurities will happen. The sooner you recognize it, the sooner you will overcome it.

"Sometimes I take a fast from makeup," Emma adds, "to take myself back to the natural part of me and to realize I don't need it. I can enjoy wearing it, but not use it as a crutch and depend on it to feel better about myself."

She continues, "Today I put on makeup the Asian way."

"The Asian way?" I ask curiously.

"It's my own phrase," she laughs. "Asians can't make their eyeshadow as big as Caucasian women. I realize I can't put on makeup like a Caucasian woman, and that's okay. Sometimes I use false eyelashes to make my eyes appear bigger, but only for special occasions, like my engagement photo shoot."

"I notice the Asian way accentuates your elegant Asian DNA," I say.

She smiles.

Could you be obsessed over your perceived imperfections? Comparison is powerful like that. It can work for you—we all compare, and some of it is good and healthy and helps us figure out who we are; or against you—some of it does very little good and even lowers self-esteem and worth. Emma needed time to grow up and into loving herself and embracing her Asian features. Can you relate? Put down the phone. Step away from the perfect selfie. You are acceptable just the way you are. Watch the Netflix original *The Social Dilemma*. It's an insightful documentary on social media, comparison, and how it undermines our security, value, and happiness.

TRUST AGAIN

IT'S WORTH THE RISK

Taking care is one way to show your love. Another way is letting people take good care of you when you need it.

MISTER ROGERS

CHAPTER 14

ONWARD

We are called to be faithful, take those first difficult steps—
and to leave the results up to God.

ALEX HARRIS

DYLAN WALKS THROUGH the door of the campus library, where I wait to meet him at the circulation desk. We had exchanged a brief email telling where to find each other and when. The library is near his dorm and convenient. When we meet, he smiles and reaches out to shake my hand. My first impression is that he is the kind of guy most everyone likes—polite, personable, and confident, with some sort of icing on top of all that. It is the "something else" that draws me in quickly, some sort of positive energy I'll get to the bottom of soon enough.

He is twenty, a transfer student from the South Side of Chicago studying finance at a small, conservative Christian college. We take the stairs to a quiet room on the top floor that I'd reserved ahead of time and are met by the usual single large table and four chairs. Dylan is between classes and tells me he is not in a hurry when we sit across from each other. I slip a paper across the table and smile, asking him to take a look at the list of fifteen or so needs adopted kids have, circle one or two, and then we'll begin. I slide over a pen. He grabs it, leans over, and begins circling and circling and circling.

He slides the paper back, as if waiting for a grade. He is eager to talk. Carefully, I scan the page. If he is going to cover all this, he has a lot on his mind.

He jumps in. "Experiences scar people. I have memories of living with my biological mom. Like, Jerry Springer–type memories."

He waits as if he needs the green light to keep going. I look up from my computer, surprised by his opening. On occasion I have accidently bumped into *The Jerry Springer Show* while flipping between stations. It's one of those grimy shows I avoid because the screaming and yelling and creepy topics turn my stomach. But Dylan is serious.

"My mom was a drug addict and an alcoholic." He begins describing how his mother's addictions destroyed their relationship. "I knew she loved and cared for me, but even at five years old, I could feel the emotional and relational disconnect."

Her hard life left her incapable of properly caring for him.

"I remember her taking me into bars while she'd get drunk. I was so young and unaware, running my Hot Wheels car around the rim of the table while she drank."

At one point, his mom got into so much trouble that they both landed in a rehab center. The good thing, he says, is that while his mom did rehab, he got to attend kindergarten. The bad thing is that three months in, his mom couldn't handle it anymore. She took him and ran away from the rehab center, and for nine months, they were on the run from the police. They would go for days without eating, hiding in alleys or couch surfing.

When the police finally caught up with them, Dylan was put into foster care.

"She had no grounds to keep me. I was the last of six kids my mom lost custody of, siblings I never knew."

Dylan barely takes a breath. He is describing some pretty raw stuff. It wasn't safe for him to be with his mom even when his foster family adopted him. His adoption was closed at first to protect him from her. During that time, he tells me, he never cried.

"I think I was already too numb from all the pain I had experienced."

On top of that, his biological father did hard drugs and wasn't capable of parenting on any level at any time.

"I reconnected with him when I turned eighteen. I could tell he wanted to be responsible, but he was not mentally there."

Today, two years later, he says his father's brain cells are nearly gone after decades on drugs. In an attempt not to judge his father's poor decision to use hard drugs, he focuses in on the consequences of dumb choices at a young age.

Dumb choices had a ripple effect on Dylan's life, like the ripples that occur from tossing a boulder into filthy swamp water. Neglect, loss of trust, feeling unwanted . . . the circles on the paper begin to appear in Dylan's story. After being on the run, hungry, without a place to call home, and unable to trust people close to him when he first arrived at his new family, he was a five-year-old mess.

"I didn't connect with anyone at first. I couldn't bring myself to trust anyone. I first warmed up to my new brothers. They felt safe, played with me, and didn't ask a bunch of questions. Even though my new mom and dad were loving and caring, I had a lot of anger issues and took it out on them."

He says he was too young to make sense of what was happening to him or put it into words. There were times when he and his family would all gather around the dinner table and play board games, and for no reason he'd snap, flipping the game board over and freaking out.

"I would smash holes in the walls for nothing too," he says.

"For nothing? Meaning you weren't provoked by a sibling?" I ask.

"No. Little things would tick me off. My anger would build up, and I'd direct it at people when it had nothing to do with them. I'd be at my worst after a visit from my birth mom. When she left, I'd turn all my anger on my new mom and scream, 'I hate you!'"

He describes his body convulsing so hard and tears pouring down his face so fast at times that he could hardly see or breathe.

"That was a ton of feelings for a young kid to take on," I whisper.

"Yeah, my new mom would calm me down over and over again. I apologized to her so many times I can't even count. Both my parents stuck by me as I detoxed from trauma."

The four walls that hold our conversation private for the moment now contain the message of a traumatized child. Mindful that he has given me a glimpse of what trauma looks like, he is quick to explain why it was so hard at first when he got adopted.

"Adjusting to a new family takes time."

"Yeah, I bet." Years of hurt and confusion can really take hold.

"It takes work to adjust to new ways of thinking. Some kids won't be able to do it."

"I've heard this before. You're saying you worked really hard at letting people in?"

"Yeah. It wasn't easy. It's easier to disconnect."

Somewhere along the way, Dylan has developed a need to talk to kids like him. He says kids with trauma find it difficult to understand or believe their new family's love is real. He's told many kids that love is when your mom makes you dinner. Love is when she gives you warm hugs. Love is a soft bed to sleep in. Most likely from experience, he adds, "Even after you call your mom or dad names and treat them like crap, they let you come home." He says if only adopted kids who struggle with trust could see, like he did, how passionate parents are about helping them.

"So what you're saying to them is, How many holes do you have to punch in the wall to fix the hole in your heart?" I ask.

"Yeah. That's what I'm saying."

"You have a voice of experience. It sounds like love is a hard concept when you've been deeply hurt and trying to reconnect with the real you?"

"It took me until I was eighteen years old to realize that I needed to get professional help. I had to figure out that asking for help is not a sign of weakness but a new light, a new perspective to help you discover yourself and who you are."

He describes learning to open up over time and with help from a psychologist friend at his church.

"The psychologist recognized that I needed help understanding my emotions."

Dylan says his brain chemistry was so messed up that the psychologist created a chart with a bunch of words on it like *flustered*, *angry*, *anxious*, and so on, to help him get a grip on his emotions. If something emotional was threatening or brewing,

Dylan was to look at the chart and point to an emotion; it helped him figure out what was going on inside.

> **EVERYONE CAN LEARN TO USE THEIR EMOTIONS IN A HEALTHIER WAY.**

Dylan had been operating on extreme emotions so long that he needed to be retaught the nuances of emotions and how they fit the situation.

"Everyone can learn to use their emotions in a healthier way," he says. "The psychologist was easy to talk to and wasn't pushy," Dylan added. "He just asked me how I felt at the time and alluded to solutions by asking the right questions."

Over time, this process helped him grow emotionally.

"It was a relief to have someone I trusted to talk with. The HIPAA,[1] a document to protect my privacy, made me feel safe without worrying he would tell my parents. Sometimes a guy just needs privacy without judgment to open up. I would recommend opening up to someone you feel the most comfortable with—someone who is genuine, caring, and trustworthy—and carefully let out what is stuck inside."

"It sounds like you made a lot of progress working with the psychologist?"

"Don't think I'm a saint," he warned.

"What do you mean?" I notice my hands are in prayer position as I lean in to rest my chin in the crook of my thumbs.

"It took me a long time to break down the wall. It took me a long time to even realize I had a wall; traumatizing events cause your brain to go into survival mode and protect you from memories. But when I did work on the walls, I found my true self."

"Do you trust others?"

"Trust is still difficult for me. I try hard and practice hard."

"That makes sense, right? Trying and practicing?"

"I still disconnect from people at times, but it happens less and less now. Connecting on an emotional level is hard for me, but it's not like it was when I first began working on it. That's proof right there that your body and brain can heal, even if sometimes it feels wrong and weird."

"You're doing it." I smile.

"Yeah. The difference is that I am willing to work hard to figure myself out so I feel secure. When I think about my five-year-old self wandering the streets in my dirty Keds and stained SpongeBob T-shirt, bellyaching, mom present but not really there, it still gets to me on some level. But it won't defeat me."

Dylan's adoptive mom and dad have been instrumental in his life. His father is a finance professional whom Dylan looks up to, and his mom is involved in community theater and their church ministries in the city. He says she's someone he admires.

Still, Dylan says, "There were times in my life I felt like no one else understood, and times I felt alone with my feelings locked inside. But I know people cared. I know God made me to be loved. He made a family to love me too. God has placed people in my life to help me notice my gifts and talents and to help me thrive. God wants that for others like me too. He wants each of us to thrive in our own way. He loves us. He wants us to do what we want to do, but under his care and for his glory."

As a Christ follower myself, I agree, noticing the Holy Spirit in me connecting on a deeper level with him. "It sounds like you are okay with giving your feelings to God?"

"Yeah. To get close to God, I don't have to be emotional or

emotionally developed. We all come to God with our own baggage he can work with. He is not always going to be loud in your life, but when you invite him in, he is there, moving, seeking, listening, available, wanting you in that moment."

Over the course of his twenty years, Dylan has endured the life of a street kid, wrestled with fear and lack of trust, learned how to vent in healthy ways, and found his way to begin again. His life is worth it. His future is bright. After college, he hopes to pay it forward and create a foundation to fund a home for kids who need a place to stay when they don't have a place to call home. He will return to the South Side of Chicago, where it all began for him. There, he hopes to help others like him; he believes if he teaches and helps other kids, they will teach and help others one day too.

I ask Dylan if I can pray for him before he races back to his dorm. He isn't weirded out. We both bow our heads, God's Spirit blessing him and his story. When we head out the door, he says, "To think I could have missed out on all this good because of the bad I once held inside so tight."

Happy, sad, angry, mad, scared . . . emotions all work well when they're in healthy balance. But trauma can cause us to get stuck in one emotion—roundabouts of endless anger or spirals of depression—and we need help getting unstuck. Lashing out or shutting down are usually a hint or clue that you need some guidance to use your full range of emotions well. If I were Dylan, and held his story inside, I'd be angry too—no, furious—about what happened to me. But furious doesn't do well long-term. It blocks you from experiencing healthy relationships. It prevents you from being you. And the world definitely needs you.

CHAPTER 15

THE OTHER SIDE OF HURT

God made you wonderful, marvelous and amazing.
And he made you on purpose.

SADIE ROBERTSON HUFF

Come home," he said through tears. "You don't belong here; you belong with us in Michigan."

Haley told me she could feel her adoptive dad's heart pounding in her ear as he hugged her close, crying.

"I had put my parents through so much, and still my mom and dad wanted nothing more than to have their daughter come home. I knew in that moment that he loved me unconditionally, even after all I had done and all I had said over the years."

Two months earlier, Haley had run away to Tennessee, where her birth mother lived, thinking she could go there and live with her after all the years of being apart.

"I felt like I had made too many bad choices with my adopted family and that they couldn't accept my faults anymore. Through my teen years, I had let them down time and time again." Shame hovered over her words.

"So I moved to Tennessee when I was eighteen years old, and of course it did not go well or as planned. Little did I realize it was just me running away from my problems again."

Haley, now twenty, a sometimes college student and full-time front-desk receptionist at a hotel chain, found me through a friend of a friend. When we spoke for the first time, she was living at home. Now she has her own apartment and lives on her own. Some people I interview are reluctant at first to talk; it's tricky business sharing your hurt. Others are, "Let's talk," as if they have been waiting to share what they have learned for the world to hear. Haley is ready to talk. The timing is right. Any sooner, she would have said no. She is learning to trust in a way she never knew was possible. As I see it, she's writing her story in the book of life so others can have hope, maybe stop running like she did. Hers is a story of trauma, neglect, fresh starts, undeserved forgiveness, and second, third, and fourth chances.

"When I was little, my birth mom and dad used drugs," she says. "I remember. They were unwilling to admit their choices were wrong or to change for the sake of my siblings and me. Even as a four-year-old, I could tell things weren't right. When they were high, they didn't act like themselves. It scared me and made me feel confused and worried. To make up for her neglect, my birth mom would buy me material things like clothes and toys. But all I wanted from her was love. So as early on as four years old, I started to run away. That's when I began the lifelong pattern of running away from my problems."

We speak in low tones about kids and trust and how she lost her own trust at an early age and couldn't get it back.

"My first interaction with trust, or broken trust, came from birth parents who neglected me emotionally and made me their last priority. A therapist once told me that every time trust is broken, even starting as a little baby, a solid brick gets layered around your heart. As every brick of broken trust adds up, it seals away your heart, trapping your pain and sorrow inside. The only way to release the hurt—to trust again—is to chip away at that brick wall."

A brick wall is a good visual. I get it. Each brick represents a time she was neglected as a wee one.

"My birth parents' neglect set me up for a lifetime of trying to rebuild real trust. By the time I was nine, I had a full wall of bricks assembled around my heart."

By nine. I ponder that. That's a lot of sorrow trapped inside someone so small. Not to mention, if the wall can keep all that in, it can keep a whole lot out. Walls act as protection from further perceived hurt. I can see where this was leading, especially when Haley tells me that, after years in the foster care system, she had lost track of how many placements she'd had. She also had a failed adoption.

"By the time I finally got adopted, I was determined not to trust my adoptive parents or be receptive to their love, no matter how hard they tried. I was not aware that I was doing this to myself and our relationship, but I was working hard at pushing my parents away from day one. Looking back, I can see that the wall surrounding my heart was sealed."

She tells me she was so sealed up that no one was getting in. No cracks. No secret passageway. Even healthy relationships were forbidden. It was her heart's primitive attempt at trying to protect itself from more hurt.

When her younger brother and sister were eventually adopted into the same family, Haley says she tried to protect them too, like a wolf protecting her young, fangs and all. She fought hard and recklessly against her parents for control. Her younger sister responded differently.

"My sister, three years younger, handled our new family much differently from me. While I was loud, she was quiet, holding everything in until she couldn't take it anymore. Then she'd cry her eyes out and lean on our parents. That was the big difference. She took the risk. I didn't—or couldn't. When she finally let go, our parents were there for her, and she learned to trust again. For me, I did the opposite. I couldn't let go. It was too risky. Trust was too foreign to me."

She confesses, "I wish I could say I got better at the whole trust thing, but that would be lying.

"The truth is, I left my adopted home at seventeen, bent on pushing my parents away forever. I thought I was so mature and knew everything. I moved in with my boyfriend, and we fell off the grid for almost two years. I was looking for love anywhere but my parents. Anybody—teachers, friends, boyfriends. I mostly wanted to fill my love gap with a boy. I learned the hard way that doesn't work when, after two years of being together, he broke my heart and I didn't have a solid reason for it."

"I'm sorry," I say. I can't imagine how alone Haley must have felt.

"I had no right to expect what happened next. When my boyfriend decided to leave me, my parents swooped in with love and compassion. Even though I had left them, after years of teenage rage and thinking they were out to do me wrong, they were still there for me. I wondered, *Is this the type of love I longed for?* But I just couldn't trust it. It was too hard. I was too messed up."

"Dang."

"Eventually I ran away again," she says. "This was my pattern. Some of us have to learn the hard way. I moved to Tennessee, to my birth mom's house. It didn't turn out well. While I was there, she got into drugs again. When she told me that it was my fault she relapsed, our relationship changed completely. I had to call my parents."

"So they didn't know where you were?" I ask.

"No. And I had to admit I had taken the car they bought."

"How did they react?"

"They were furious. Who wouldn't be? My dad took the first flight he could get to Tennessee to pick up the car. When he arrived, I fully intended to stay—until he broke down, and I saw the hurt and love he had for me."

I can't help thinking that her dad's loving actions were making a dent in that brick fortress she had spoken of earlier.

"You went home?"

"Yes. I had been running away for so long, I just needed to go home and deal with my messy self. So I went home with him."

"What a relief." The words slip out of my mouth.

LITTLE THINGS [LIKE JOURNALING] HELP ME LET MY GUARD DOWN.

She continues. "Now that I am twenty, I can see how the rage and distrust had clouded my vision. When I was younger, I couldn't see any of it. And while I have many regrets for what I did and how I behaved then, I don't know what I could have done differently during that time of struggling with painful trust issues. To find myself again and trust again was an up-and-down journey of rebuilding trust. Thankfully, today I feel like I am on the other side of hurt. One thing that helps is journaling. It's odd. You can scream on paper instead of screaming in people's faces and feel relief. Sometimes I write letters to people

I miss who are not part of my life anymore. It helps. Little things like this help me let my guard down. With my guard down now, I can see everything my parents have done for me. I can finally see the proof of their love.

"My parents and I have a relationship today because the brick wall is slowly coming down," she admits. "I trust more than ever."

Her parents have helped her out of spots so tight and dark she was sure she was lost. Over and over they reached down, grabbed her hand, and pulled her out of the fortress she'd built for herself.

"What would you say to teens who are struggling with letting their guard down?" I ask.

"Maybe you need to take the hand extended out to you, grab on, and feel the pull back into a life where you can rediscover that it is okay to trust again. Being older makes a big difference too. I still struggle today, but on a much smaller scale. I guess I'm more self-aware and able to realize when I'm self-sabotaging. Forgiveness was key for me, and realizing you can't hold on to things forever. God helps people through good and hard times. That's the reason I'm telling my story, and I hope it can help somebody else who might be going through something like this."

What does your wall look like? Some are short and scalable. The tall ones? No one is getting in. Have you considered yours? Trauma can change the way you trust. If you lost trust at an early age due to trauma, you know your wall. But don't lose heart. Breaking down walls is a process that is doable, but it takes being intentional. You have to be all in, and that means walking alongside someone who has the tools and know-how to help you chip away at that wall of protection.

CHAPTER 16

FROM OVERWHELMED TO WEDDING BELLS

Some people care too much. I think it's called love.

A. A. MILNE

SARA IS AN outgoing twenty-five-year-old with a lot going on in her life, and she likes it that way. When we speak, she and her husband had spent the morning turkey hunting in the woods but had tramped out empty-handed when snowflakes filled the April air. The young couple bowhunt too, a skill Sara learned as a teen while visiting her brother's foster family. Add archery league (which she describes as like a bowling league, only you aim at targets, not pins), deer hunting (her husband more than her), making homemade jerky in dehydrators, and grinding their own burgers. Of course I'm impressed, but even more so when she adds that they both have jobs, a baby, and are in the midst of remodeling their first home.

We lose ourselves in a side conversation about homemade biscuits and gravy, and she laughs when I ask if she's ever considered exchanging water for 7UP when she's whipping up a batch of dough. "It makes the biscuits extra fluffy," I say. She's willing to give it a try.

Sara's living her dream and loving life in spite of the complicated and broken road she traveled to arrive here. But she says she wouldn't be where she is today without the support and love of her adoptive family. She tells me she was fostered first and then adopted. So I ask, "What were you like in foster care?"

"I didn't do well as a teen in foster care in their home. Looking back on it, I was the hardest kid living in the home."

It's hard to believe after our sweet conversation and bonding over biscuits and gravy.

Then she tells me she struggled with mother figures, and she didn't connect well with her first mom.

"My mom had me when she was sixteen."

As a newborn, Sara went to live with her grandparents.

"I don't recall a hundred percent how long I lived with them, but during all those years, I rarely saw my mom."

So she didn't attach to her mom. Over the years, her mom showed up less and less.

When Sara was eight, her mom randomly showed up one day and took her to live with her and two brothers Sara didn't even know she had. After that, every day was unpredictable. She floated between home and her Nana's house. The bright spot? Playing with her brothers. But by the time she turned eleven, her life had become a blur of watching her younger brothers and getting supper on the table.

"I felt like I just couldn't be a kid."

When her mom wasn't around, and that was often, Sara was the mom.

"So you never developed trust in your mom?" I ask.

"No."

"It sounds like your days were unpredictable."

Sara nods. "I was really hurt. She made some bad choices."

The unpredictability continued when the cops showed up the day her mom lost custody of the kids. That day, the three siblings were divided between three different foster homes. For Sara, it was overwhelming and scary.

"I was in seventh grade. It was just after spring break. I worried about my brothers all the time."

She finished seventh and eighth grades in her first placement.

"I rarely saw my brothers," she says.

Then one of her brothers was placed in a new foster family after the first family moved to Texas. Sara remembers the tide turned when her brother was adopted.

"While all this was happening, his new family fought to foster me too, to keep my brother and me together."

I smile. "I love the word 'fought.' It's significant. They fought for you and won!"

"Yes. I lived with Tim and Judy from the end of eighth grade to graduation from high school and before I moved on campus at college."

> **LEARNING TO TRUST AGAIN WAS LIKE RELEARNING HOW TO WALK AND TALK.**

But it wasn't all Krispy Kreme Doughnuts. Sara was happy to be placed in a family with her brother, but she was angry with her bio mom for constantly lying that she would get them back. I sense she carried her leery anger into her new family along with her suitcase, wondering who would hurt her next. I imagine it was hard to trust again so quickly.

She tells me it was especially hard for her to trust her new foster mom.

"I had never experienced a nurturing relationship with my mom, and I was so upset with her, so I didn't know how to get along with my new foster mom, who was very nurturing."

Sara says her first mom wasn't there for her when she needed her most. The difference is, her new mom *was* there when she needed her most, but Sara didn't know how to accept this kind of love. Instead, she needed to feel in control to feel safe. The risk of being hurt again was too high. Learning to trust again was like relearning how to walk and talk. So in what I'd call a self-defense response, she pushed away her adoptive mom and any attempts to connect, and instead kept her distance.

"I had taken care of myself for so long, I thought I didn't need anyone taking care of me," she says.

Like most parents do, her new mom and dad tried to guide her through high school and dating with healthy boundaries to keep her safe.

"But all I felt was them keeping me from doing what I wanted to do, like date boys."

Sara remembers a guy who was nothing but trouble.

"My parents kept telling me to stay away from him, but I wouldn't listen. Looking back, they were right. I should have listened. I was pretty hardheaded and hard on them. But they didn't give up on me. Even when I screwed up and didn't listen to them, they would sit down and talk about it with me. They would pray with me. Dad would open up and tell me about his screw-ups as a young man and how he had turned his life around, how it took trusting God for everything to change. That's why my parents didn't hold my screw-ups over my head. They had experienced forgiveness and wanted me to experience the healing forgiveness can bring too."

"They believed in you?"

"Yes. Even though I came from a hard upbringing and gave my foster parents hell as a teen, they believed in me and still do. They saw a strong young lady. Their love is relentless. Our relationship has grown so much. I call them Mom and Dad because they feel like my mom and dad. They came into my life when I needed them most and raised me when my mom was not healthy."

Sara says her early childhood trauma is part of her, and she still struggles today, although less and less.

"I am always working on it," she says. "If you are one of the lucky ones who got a great adoptive home like I did, enjoy it. Give them a chance. Don't screw it up. I know what it's like to be new in a home—it's hard. You only think about yourself and about trying to survive. But I overcame my struggles, with so much support. I am in a good place now."

Shortly after college, something holy and beautiful took place. Sara got married.

On a gorgeous, warm summer day, after pictures with the wedding party at the family farm, the blushing bride arrived at the church met by two dads: her biological dad, a man who had mostly been in and out of her life and was never a stable figure, and Tim, her adoptive dad, who had always been there for her. On this day the complexities of life would vanish.

"I took my adopted dad's arm on the right and my birth dad's arm on the left, and together the one who brought me into the world and the one who shepherded me through walked me down the aisle."

That day, both dads gave her away. Then her adopted dad, Tim, took his place at the front, clutched his Bible in his hand, and as tears streamed down their faces, he performed the wedding ceremony, and Kurtis and Sara were married.

"That night we celebrated as one big happy family," Sara says, "I split my father-daughter dance with both dads."

I sigh.

"Today I am twenty-five, married, and have an eight-month-old baby boy. Tim and Judy are a huge part of our lives. They will always be Mom and Dad to me, and I could not ask for better grandparents for our son."

I'd say she's arrived.

What I've learned from Sara is that the ability to trust, once lost, can be restored, especially in the presence of good people who care and consistently show themselves trustworthy, patient, and forgiving. Huddled with her mom and dad in prayer, Sara found restoration for her shattered trust, healing for her heart, and the ability both to receive forgiveness and to forgive.

CHAPTER 17

LEARNING HOW TO LIVE AGAIN

We . . . we . . . weren't blank pages, were we?

SAROO BRIERLY

THERE IS SURVIVING, and there is living," Elise explains in a quiet voice, barely audible above the coffee-shop chatter. "Surviving is getting through each day and night, one thing at a time. You experience it and get over it. Living is more like you are free. You can do what you want; you can fly like a bird, like an eagle. I like to picture myself as an eagle. Nothing to stop you, just flying high."

Elise, twenty-five, never expected she'd need to learn how to live again. Doesn't one just live? Doesn't life just happen, like, happily ever after and all? Not so much. Especially when you're battling skeletons in your birth family closet, like the ones that have haunted Elise most of her life.

No, just surviving was not how she wanted to live for the rest of her life. She had to be free.

Elise, a college student who also works full-time in manufacturing, is dressed in Nike sweats and a hoodie. She tells me she is an introvert who is pretty shy and doesn't like attention. I ask why.

"Because you have to explain yourself," she says. "Expressing myself—I struggle with that."

Besides being an introvert, Elise says she thrives on routine. Routine is comfortable.

Elise was born in Russia in 1994, shortly after the fall of the Soviet Union. She was born in Nizhny Novgorod, an approximately 250–mile train ride from Moscow. She grew up in and out of orphanages, mostly in, until she was nine. Her early memories are vivid but spotty, a combination of her own and those told to her by her older biological sister, Sara, who was also adopted by an American family and lives about two hours away.

Sara, the keeper of memories, remembers when their mom was a good mom and had a good job before she went to jail for five years. Sara explained to Elise that their mom wasn't a killer, but in self-defense she had killed her boyfriend, a bad guy who would have killed her. That's when the girls were placed in two different orphanages. Elise, a baby at the time, doesn't remember when her mom went to jail. But she vividly remembers an orphanage for autism where she was wrongly placed and lived for five years, "just being alone and surviving."

When she and her mom were reunited, they were never the same again. Elise was five. Jail had changed them both. She believes depression pulled her mom into alcohol, then neglect. And that neglect pulled Elise into fear, then silence. Trauma will do that.

"I was a baby. I was in the wrong orphanage. My mother was in jail," she softly says, as if saying it too loudly will make it happen again. "I kept asking myself, Why did this person who was supposed to watch over me not watch over me? She didn't teach me anything. I got the worst end of the deal. You don't party and drink alcohol [in front of a child]. I watched all that. Why did she choose that life over me?"

Elise's backstory is important for her story to make sense. She lost more than her mom at an early age; she lost her sense of security, comfort, and trust, the very bearings that make one feel safe and whole. The hurt reflects in her soft-spoken voice. I keep quiet, holding my teacup close to my lips, sipping, listening, thinking, believing that the more she talks about her trauma, the more likely she will disarm its power over her.

I wonder, as her story unfolds, how a person who seemingly lost everything ever finds security, comfort, and trust again. Is it even possible?

Fast-forward to 2004. Elise, nine going on ten, was placed back in a different orphanage, one of forty or so in Nizhny. One day, she says, she was offered a strange opportunity: to attend camp in the United States. Not a YMCA camp or wilderness camp but a two-week camp with a host family.

"At that time, my parents were looking to adopt. My original host family had canceled, so the coordinator contacted my parents."

"What was it like living with a foreign family?" I ask.

"I could not speak English, so it was a struggle to communicate. But it was freeing and fun. I got toys and got to meet my parents' extended family."

"Did you want to be adopted?"

"Who would say no to adoption when you are this little kid who received toys and got to swim and explore the world? I definitely said yes, and the translator told my parents that I was interested, and so were they."

What sounded like a match made in heaven was far from

it. Unbeknownst to her new parents, Elise came with a hole in her heart the size of the Grand Canyon. She didn't know how to be in a family or to accept love. Her patterns of protection were carved too deep for a quick transformation. Likewise, her family didn't know how to navigate a hurt little girl. Unlike Annie in the musical, who makes a complete transformation, Elise was more lost than ever.

Over the next ten years, ages nine to nineteen, she admits she felt like she didn't fit into her family. Elise wanted to be normal, even craved normal, but couldn't figure out what normal was. Although she was extremely shy in school and more easily made friends with teachers, she did find a few friends her age, played sports, and played on the playground. But at home she was hard to live with. She says her emotions were so hidden that her parents had a hard time understanding her and what she wanted. Academics were tough and frustrating too. Overwhelmed and anxious, at home Elise morphed into an edgy statue of silence.

"I was a statue when it came to confrontations or conflict; there were no words that came out and no tears. I had no expression on my face at all, so they couldn't read how I was feeling or if I understood what they were saying. I did not use words to hurt them, but my silence hurt them. I was silent when my parents got frustrated and yelled at me. My mom especially was hurt by the silence and would get mad."

Elise says she would leave for long walks after her parents gave up trying to talk to her. "I was trying to protect myself so what happened to me in the past wouldn't happen again."

"So you needed to feel safe, but to feel safe you had to be in control, and to be in control meant—"

"It meant I would not say a single thing and just stand there and listen. I also kept everyone at bay to protect them and myself. I never lashed out, but I started to talk back when I was nineteen. I sure didn't give any affection. I didn't like hugs. My parents didn't know what to do, so they stood back. My aunts kept hugging me, and I'd try to pull away, but they kept doing it, and eventually I gave in. Parents should keep doing it until their child gives in."

I nod. "Sounds like good advice. What did you learn from the hugs?"

"Not everyone is out there to hurt you," she answers.

"That's huge."

"Yeah. I slowly let them in."

But not her parents. Elise and her parents were all feeling out of control and misunderstood.

Even if her parents had known what to do, tried their hardest, showed unconditional love, Elise—or let's say the scared, enraged girl inside her—probably would have refused their love. And she did.

"I was at the end of my string and trying to cut it off," she says.

I take a deep breath and quickly review our conversation in my head. She couldn't cry—a clear indicator she didn't know how to grieve her traumatic childhood to release the sorrow inside. She couldn't shake the past that was shaking her. She had refused her parents' attempts to understand her. I'm relieved when she tells me that at age nineteen she signed herself into a mental health hospital.

"Watching and learning from others at Pine Rest helped me to realize I was not the only one who struggles," she says. "The people there helped me see I didn't want to be stuck in a stage of suffering for the rest of my life. They helped me set goals. I didn't like the way I was feeling all the time. I am taking medicine for anxiety and depression now. Life is a whole new adventure, and I have a new perspective."

She adds, "I also learned that maybe my parents react because I react."

"That's insightful," I admit. Later I trace through my notes and recognize how much pain was simmering under the surface. How everyone involved was in the dark. How Elise's acting out was a message that was hard for her parents to decipher, almost like a foreign Morse code. Wars have started for similar reasons. No wonder.

After being hospitalized, Elise moved home again. But by twenty-one she moved out, unable to adapt. This was the first of several move-out attempts.

"The first time, my parents kicked me out because I was acting ridiculous and wasn't working with them," she says. "The second time I moved out, I wanted independence, and I was scared of being kicked out again. The third time I moved out was perfect. I had a better relationship with my parents, and they were always so helpful. I just had a hard time accepting help. I thought I could do it all on my own. But I believe my parents wanted to help."

"Me too," I smile.

She continues, "My dad never understood what it feels like to struggle the way I have. He's had a pretty good life. My mom had a rough road growing up, so she understands what it is like to struggle."

"It only takes one to start a connection," I say.

But she found more too: a connection with God.

"Our pastor was preaching about changing yourself," she explains. "He said you have to change yourself before you can expect anyone else to change. Change yourself first, he said. I didn't understand it right away. But I thought, if I change myself, my parents will change. At first nothing changed. It was slow. But over time I've learned to accept my parents, and they are learning to accept me."

She laughs and reassures me, "My parents do like me."

I laugh too. "I believe you. You got me liking you, and we just met."

She smiles. "I have always been interested in why I do things and act the way I do. Like why I shut down. Why don't my parents see my soul? I like psychology. When I had troubles with my parents that I couldn't understand, I wanted to learn more about what was going on."

"You arrived scared and enraged to the point you couldn't show affection to your parents, you couldn't connect. They were scared for you," I point out.

> " I HAD TO FORGIVE MYSELF FOR THE PERSON I USED TO BE BECAUSE I AM NOT THAT PERSON ANYMORE. I AM BETTER THAN I USED TO BE. I AM A BETTER VERSION OF MYSELF TODAY.

She nods. "I couldn't control it. I was little. It hurt them and it hurt me. I have had to forgive myself for the drinking, acting out, not listening to my parents. I had to forgive myself for the person I used to be because I am not that person anymore. I am better than I used to be. I am a better version of myself today."

It gets better. It gets easier. I am relieved, thrilled actually, ready to reach across the table and hug her for her vulnerability, for sharing the truth. It does get better. It does.

"Forgiveness helps," she adds.

"Forgiveness has the power to heal and set us free," I say.

"Yes. But it doesn't stop there."

"No? What do you mean?"

"At this point in my life, I reflect and think and ask myself, how have I grown? If you don't want change, nothing will come from it. You have to want it! No one else can do it for you."

She continues, "I have a relationship with God. It's kinda weird. Sometimes it's like, 'Help me out here!' Other times it's, 'Okay, I'm good.' I finally figured out he's going to be in your life no matter what. Even if you don't believe, know that someone has your back, you are being watched over. I feel safer knowing God is with me."

"Your story is so raw and vulnerable."

"It's a story. I can't change it. You don't get over it fully . . . you get through it. I like who I am today, and I continue to work on liking myself more each day and night."

"And who would you say you are today?" I ask.

"Silly, smart, understanding of others, compassionate. I have opportunities, friends, a good job, and I am going to school for engineering," she says with a smile. "I am learning how to live again."

Some teens—and young adults—don't know why they act out and do what they do. At twenty-five, Elise is able to look back on her teen years with clarity and piece together what was going on. She says to all the teens out there, don't wait. Choose to work on yourself. No one can do it for you. Explore what's going on inside before you hurt yourself and the ones you love. It's possible to really live, not just survive.

CHAPTER 18

PUTTING IT INTO WORDS

When we talk about our feelings, they become less overwhelming, less upsetting, and less scary.

MISTER ROGERS

FOR THE LONGEST time Ana struggled to talk about her feelings of abandonment. It felt scary and uncomfortable. It was all too uncertain. If she talked, what would she say? "Hey, I've got abandonment issues"? Honestly, Ana didn't even know she had abandonment issues.

Until one day she skimmed *The Primal Wound* by Nancy Verrier, a book about why adoptees do what they do. Her mom was digging through it for insight. Ana says she found it lying on the counter in their kitchen. Every line was eye-opening, like the pages were talking to her, just her. That's when she began to put two and two together: she had underlying, unresolved issues of abandonment that were keeping her from healthy relationships—not so much with her dad but with her mom and even her boyfriend.

I am sitting down with both mom and daughter to sort through the unsorted. Mainly, that Ana's relationship with her mom, Jamie, has been tense and strained from the get-go, since Ana was ten months old. Jamie filled me in.

"Ever since Ana was little—even before she came home from Guatemala—I have wanted to connect with her on that deep mother-daughter level I experienced with my own mom growing up. I pined for her over the ten months from when we were matched until I held her in my arms for the first time. You can imagine my dismay when she chose her dad over me! Even after her allegiance shifted to me when she was around four, she always managed to keep me at arm's length. *I'll let you in—but only this much.* And if I suggested it or liked it, then she rejected it. I've had to work very hard at forging connection points with Ana over the years; we share a love of many of the same foods, dining out, travel, and dogs. And every once in a while, she will lift the curtains on what I call 'the real Ana' and give me a peek inside. Those are the moments I live for and collect like treasured beach glass."

Ana was born in rural Guatemala, in the small village of El Progreso, just north of Guatemala City, the capital. But curiously, she's actually Nicaraguan, which accounts for her height. She's five foot eight, too tall to be native Guatemalan. She's a Latin American beauty with an independent streak a mile long and a reserved disposition, meaning she reserves the right to keep to herself. I laugh when I hear all this, but am quick to reconsider when I see her serious brow. She does keep to herself unless she's with friends. She also rejects YouTube makeup tutorials, preferring a natural look. Today she's pulled her long, lush brown hair with fresh highlights into a messy bun, touched up her eyebrows, and wears an oversized sweatshirt and leggings.

Ana likely spent her first ten months of life in Guatemala snuggled in a *cargador*, a simple Guatemalan blanket wrapped around her foster mother's upper body. In Guatemala, mothers wear their babies close to their heart. That way the baby feels safe and mom can tote her everywhere in close comfort. You might see where this is going.

> ## FOR SOME ADOPTEES, UNRESOLVED LOSS HOLDS THEM BACK FROM EMBRACING THE LOVE OF OTHERS.

When Ana was adopted by a Michigan couple with two older sons, her mom remembers holding her for the first time—a very petite, somber, not smiley little girl with big eyes that studied her new parents with weary caution and confusion. Jamie says the handover between the foster family and them in the hotel was intense, followed by days of screaming. Looking back, Jamie realizes Ana was trying to communicate her sorrow over losing her family. For days, Jamie says, she rocked Ana, held her, and tried to soothe her fears. In Ana's case, the separation and loss was so intense that her baby-self simply refused to accept her new family, and unresolved loss remains a part of her to this day.

For some adoptees, unresolved loss holds them back from embracing the love of others. That's what happened to Ana, and she didn't get over it. She says she has struggled emotionally ever since because she is afraid of losing someone precious again. It was too painful. So she has rarely let people in for seventeen years.

None of this is easy for Ana to talk about. When I first asked her to share her story, she avoided me for months—like, from February to July. But I was patient, and I kept praying she would get there in her head and heart and find a way to say what she'd been feeling for years. There were times, sitting in the family's living room as I always did when visiting her mom, when I'd get a quick "hey" from Ana and watch her dig into the fridge for something to eat, then disappear down the stairs and out of sight.

But now, finally, six months of waiting has paid off. Ana agrees to talk. I bring the Starbucks, and her mom joins us around their farmhouse dining table near their kitchen, the hub of gluten-free meals and grilled leftovers. At eighteen, Ana is heading to community college in the fall to explore a few career options. By explore, I mean she doesn't know what she wants to do at this point. But most of all, she says she wants to get an apartment with friends once she saves enough money.

The three of us settle in and cradle our warm cups while Zayla, the family dog, clasps a Frisbee between her teeth and relentlessly begs for a toss. It's Frisbee time all the time for Zayla; the puppy in her doesn't understand that coffee and tea are our dog treats.

Fifteen minutes into our conversation, Ana is more relaxed. We are all in a coffee daze. Our conversation flows organically like a raft floating down a lazy river. I let her lead. She tells me about her leg surgeries first.

"I am only eighteen and I have had multiple surgeries; most because I was born with legs that had issues. I don't know how to explain it . . . knock-knee, I guess, which means my knees were turned in, and my feet too."

She pulls out her iPhone to show me the before-and-after X-rays of her legs. The white, ghostly images faintly reveal her warped bones turned in at the knees. I study the images and see the distorted bones and wonder how she managed to play sports or even walk.

"How did you play soccer?" I ask curiously, knowing she played on a club team.

"I cried myself to sleep," she says.

Her mom looks at her with wide eyes. "You never told me this before!"

The two spend a few moments thinking back, trying to remember the specifics. Ana recalls walking weirdly, as she puts it, and how it started affecting her hips. By third grade, she remembers the pain felt like knives stabbing her little legs. She recalls lots of cramping, always on the left. Doctors were baffled. By sixth grade she was in so much pain she shouldn't have been able to play soccer—but she did because she loved it, she says.

At the same time, she became more vocal about her increasing aches and pains, and her mom got more assertive, chasing hard after answers on the internet like a fox chasing a rabbit. Every twist and turn through medical articles brought her closer to much-needed answers. Finally, her determination landed them at the Cleveland Clinic in Ohio, with a real diagnosis and mixed emotions. Ana would need multiple surgeries, requiring months of recovery in casts, braces, crutches, and wheelchairs, for years.

Looking back, Ana adds, "If I hadn't been adopted, those surgeries most likely would've never happened. I wouldn't want to imagine what type of pain and messed up legs I would have lived with as a child in Guatemala. I am extremely thankful I was adopted."

And she means it—like, *really* means it. She knows she would have always been in pain. But it's uncomfortable to say thank you, she says, especially to her family.

"Being thankful for being adopted is complicated."

"Why?" I ask.

"I struggle with abandonment. I have an irrational fear of being abandoned again. It's just always there, a voice in my head."

And like that, our conversation turns to abandonment. This she is nervous to talk about because she's going somewhere new and taking us with her, away from her leg scars to the scars on her heart.

"Adoption makes sense. It's great to be adopted," she says. "But there's this other side of it. I don't think people are aware of it."

"What other side?" I ask.

She slowly pieces together her thoughts.

"When a baby grows in the mother's womb," she says, "a bond and attachment forms between the mother and child. Once she is born, if separated too soon, she knows it. The separation can lead to a sense of abandonment, which may affect her when she's older."

"And this happened to you?" I ask. "You somehow know. You experience the fear of being abandoned, even today?"

"Yes." Ana nods. "But I would rather have abandonment issues than live in a third-world country making a dollar a day as a domestic, like my birth mother did, and unable to walk and in pain."

The image is hauntingly hopeless.

"So it sounds like you'd rather have abandonment issues than be totally abandoned?"

The three of us are silent, taking in the weight of the question. Then Ana responds.

"I think a lot of adopted people have abandonment issues."

"I think so too," I nod. Ana's mom agrees.

Then I ask, "What does abandonment look like for you?"

She pauses and thinks about it.

"It's like, if you try to connect to people and those people disappear, or walk out of your life, it hits you a lot harder. I was given up, and even though I know it's a poverty thing, it affects the way I let people in. I lost my first birth family, then my foster family. When I was in middle school, two of my best friends moved away and changed schools. It was hard."

"That would be hard for any kid, but you took it even harder, you're saying."

"Yes. When people leave, it triggers a deep-down feeling of loss and rejection and uncertainty. Thankfully, my family understands my abandonment tendencies," she adds.

I look at her mom across the table and wonder, does she understand? Her eyes are locked on Ana.

"What abandonment tendencies?" I ask Ana.

She explains, "I don't really show that I'm thankful to my family. It's a part of my guard. I don't show how happy I am either, because it can be taken away from me."

"What would it be like if you did?"

"If I show emotion to my family, I have an irrational fear that they will be taken away from me," Ana admits. "It feels like I am giving too much of myself. Even saying I am thankful for dinner makes me feel anxious; I don't know if I'll be accepted. It's a protective measure. I don't want to get too close and give them more of me, because if the connection is ever lost, it is too painful. I poured everything into my foster family and lost them. So I don't want to lose my family today. I am thankful and love my family, and I may not say it, but it is in there."

"I believe it's in there too."

I look over and tears are streaming down her mom's face as years of confusion finally make sense. Will things change? Time will tell. Understanding definitely opens the door to the possibility.

"Oh, Ana," her mom says, "I wish I would have known sooner. It all makes sense now. It wasn't me and you; it was the fear of losing us, our family, all over again."

While Jamie is blown away, and frankly I am too, I watch them closely. Ana doesn't say it, but I can tell she's happy she and her mom finally understand each other. Her face shows it. For the first time, she found the words to admit out loud that she lives with an irrational fear of losing people she loves. She is afraid of emotional betrayal. But it is no longer a secret hidden in her heart and no longer a secret to everyone she loves.

The way I see it, any time you shine light into darkness, it is always easier to see. Even the smallest flame in the darkest cave brings comfort. Otherwise, walking around in the dark, you keep running into the same things over and over again. That's what Ana has been doing for years. Bumping around in the dark—until now.

Jamie reaches for Ana with her words.

"Our lives didn't start out together, Ana, but I didn't think it would be different. I just thought I would love you no matter what. I often suspected you had some abandonment issues. I didn't want to label you. I thought it would subside."

Ana takes in her mom's words but doesn't respond. It will take time, more conversations, and more understanding. Today is just the beginning.

Her mom sneaks in one last question as Zayla now lies patiently, still waiting to play Frisbee. "As you mature, are you starting to realize love lasts? Or is it something you still question?"

"Both," Ana says thoughtfully.

We sit in silence, each of us thinking about this breakthrough. Ana's aha moment is an aha moment for any teen or young adult who can't fully connect with his or her parents. Struggling to attach to adoptive parents is legit for some. Ana has felt something was off her entire life; her mom felt it too. Ana's confession was brave and insightful, and she found out her honesty didn't cost her a thing when all along she thought it would. What helped Ana begin letting go of her irrational fears can help you too. Talk. Formulate your feelings and thoughts into words. You will feel exposed and uncomfortable at first, and your entire being may physically protest, like it did for Ana. But if she can open up, so can you. You are not alone.

CHAPTER 19

THE MUSIC RETURNS

I believe in the sun even when it's not shining.
I believe in love even when I don't feel it.
I believe in God even when he is silent.

ANONYMOUS JEWISH POEM WRITTEN DURING THE HOLOCAUST

How DOES A girl shattered by childhood trauma sing again when there was so little music for such a long time? I mean not just singing in the shower, or alone with AirPods, or Beats, or noise-canceling headphones, but singing praise to God in front of large audiences—a little like Taylor Swift, but on a smaller scale.

I found out when I met twenty-five-year-old Marisa. She was adopted by her foster family when she was twelve and given a permanent safe place to land and a new start. But before that, all she knew was a scramble of fear and rejection from her biological mom that lodged deep in her mind and heart like a shard of glass. She had a lot to learn about what was normal and what wasn't. Overcoming eleven years of trauma and neglect would be no small feat. Then something extraordinary happened. Somewhere along her crumbling, rocky road of a childhood and her teen years, she discovered she could sing. Like, *really* sing. Marisa believes God gave her this gift to bring back her joy.

Why does music matter? I wanted to find out. So Marisa and I arranged to meet at her office, where she works full-time at an auto repair shop, answering phones and scheduling appointments for clients. A month or so earlier, she had emailed me to talk about her childhood—the chaos, her fears, the trauma, whivh led to anxiety and hopeless depression. But with that email, she also sent me a link to watch her perform and listen to her sing. And when she sings, she is transformed.

When I arrive at her office, she is wearing a muted-yellow dress paired with strappy wedge shoes. She has a phone to her ear and motions me in with a wave as she finishes the call. I sit on an overstuffed brown couch with coffee stains and wait.

Marisa is slipping me in on her morning break. When she finally sits, I don't know what to expect. This much I know: Marisa has come out of a rough situation. With her history of trauma, she could be somebody emotionally withdrawn. She could be someone unable to make sense of what had happened to her. But she is none of those things. She is a professional young lady who makes a whole lot of sense, despite the senseless things that happened to her while growing up. And she wants to use her story to help others overcome like her.

"From the moment I can remember, there was discord in our home," Marisa begins her story. "Our house was always loud. There was always a lot of fighting and loud yelling. My mom is bipolar, violent, and mentally unstable. She's a pathological liar too. One time she shaved off her eyebrows and told us she had cancer."

"Seriously?" I ask, a bit startled.

"Oh, yes."

She would be kind sometimes. Like when her dad died, her

mom let the girls pick out a stuffed animal from the hospital gift shop to remember him by.

"What was his name?" I ask.

"Green Bear." She smiles like a little girl. But the smile quickly fades when a haunting memory surfaces. Her mother's good moments never stayed. They were inevitably followed by a shift—an angry, ugly, terrifying descent in mood and personality.

"For years she would scream things like, 'Who do you love more, your dad or me?' One time when we were riding in the car, we didn't answer her, and she ripped my sister's bear out of her hands and whipped it out the window. Then screamed even louder."

"How scary." I image Marisa as a frightened little girl gripping Green Bear with her two little fists to her chest.

"She eventually stopped the car in the middle of the road, got out, and went to get it."

I start to see the unpredictable bipolar pattern—kindness, rage, kindness, rage.

"After my dad died when I was four, we moved schools a lot. Each time, I lost my friends. I have no childhood memories like other kids do. When I was seven, my mom moved us to the other side of the state. She had nobody except her best friend, who lived over there."

"What was it like after the move?"

"It was the worst it had ever been," she says. "One day, when I was seven, my mom started throwing things at my sister and me. I was hysterical and called 911. I'm sure the person on the other end couldn't understand a word I was saying. I was so afraid. My sister and I ran to the neighbors and waited for the cops. When the cops arrived, we quickly put some clothes in a trash bag. Mom sat on my bedroom floor, sorting through and folding everything she had just thrown."

I wonder when she noticed the girls were gone.

Marisa describes riding in the back seat of the cop car to their foster home. Over the years, the girls were victims of emotional, physical, and sexual abuse. They went back and forth between home and foster care. There were a lot of school changes, sometimes leaving in the middle of the year. She says she always lost friends.

I think about her lovey Green Bear. "Was Green Bear with you?" I ask, hopeful.

"Always," she smiles.

We both get a little nostalgic about our stuffed animals and how they keep us safe. Green Bear is her closest reliable friend.

Eventually, she says, her mom became so dangerous the authorities hid the locations of their foster homes to keep the girls safe.

"My mom couldn't know where we lived. I couldn't be in yearbooks because of safety concerns," she says. It is, apparently, not uncommon for foster kids to not be in public photographs of any kind.

I didn't know about the yearbook thing. Ugh. But I get it, sort of. Safety first. My mind wanders. How hard it would be adjusting to new schools and making new friends, only to say goodbye over and over again! I imagine Marisa as a second grader, then a third grader, and year after year with no security or sense of safety.

Marisa continues filling me in. Just when the sisters thought they were safe in their new placement, her mom hired a private investigator to find them. "I saw you playing," her mom would coo during supervised visits.

Marisa explains that the caseworker couldn't hear her mom because she could only watch from behind a two-way mirror.

"I was terrified," Marisa says. "She knew what I was wearing and saw me playing with other kids in an open field near my foster home."

That's scary. But even scarier is that she watched the girls after they were adopted.

"I became paranoid and on edge," Marisa admits.

"I would too," I offer.

She knew her mom drove a Jeep Cherokee; if she saw one, she'd duck down and hide or look the other way.

"It took me ten years to get over it."

"When did you figure out your mom was mentally unstable?" I ask.

"I didn't realize how severe her instability was until high school. She was wishy-washy, but sometimes she was a great mom. We always had food. But she was emotionally absent. She didn't want me, over and over again."

"But you kept going back. I get that, I think. You wanted someone of your own."

"Yes," Marisa nods. "One time, when I was older, I tried to go back and live with my mom. It didn't work out.

"Six months later, I went back to my foster family. My sister was gone. I was super confused; I thought we'd be together again. Now I was really alone. Kids were coming and going. In foster care, kids come from everywhere. Not having my sister there was really difficult. Without her, I became very depressed.

It was one of the darkest times of my life. I made secret suicide attempts. I thought about *it* day after day. No one would miss me, I thought. I was alone."

With her sister gone, Marisa was extremely depressed. Her teen years wavered between normal thoughts, suicidal thoughts, and ongoing mental health issues. She and I talk about kids who experience trauma and the toxic effects. How they tend to isolate and get lost in their fears, thinking there is no way to escape the destructive thoughts.

One day, she got the good news. She could go live with her sister.

"Did you go?"

"Of course I did," she says, as if I'm crazy to think she wouldn't. "I'm like . . . I don't have my dad, and I really didn't have my mom. I wanted what I could get. I filled a trash bag with my stuff and went to live with my sister at her foster home."

Around the same time, Marisa says her mom's parental rights were terminated. Soon after, the sisters were adopted by their foster family.

"I was twelve. We were adopted in 2007. I was absolutely elated. My family is amazing. I had begged them to adopt me before the process even began." She smiles.

"Did their strength help hold you together?

She shakes her head no.

"Quite the opposite. They shared their own mistakes. Their vulnerability made me realize I wasn't alone in what I was feeling. That's what convinced me to keep moving forward."

But Marisa's sister got pregnant and moved out. Things got pretty dark again for Marisa. The emotional, physical, and sexual abuse she experienced as a little girl continued haunting her. Things would get worse before they got better.

"I had just gotten her back, and she was gone. She left."

"You must have felt so alone."

Again Marisa had suicidal thoughts and made secret attempts on her life that no one knew about.

As high school approached, she says she ran from her problems. She hung out with kids who didn't care about school.

"School just wasn't a priority for them. But they were my friends. If I called them today, we could pick up where we left off. They were great people with wonderful hearts who just made poor choices at the time."

She did too, she says.

"But I learned from my poor decisions and made sure it didn't happen again."

"Did you try to abandon yourself in high school?" I carefully ask.

"Yes," she says without hesitation. She's very frank.

"What changed your mind?"

"My senior year of high school. I was sitting in church, and my pastor said suicide is not a normal thought. And I said to myself, *What!* I always thought it was normal for someone to have absolutely no regard for their own life. It's something I've dealt with since I was six years old. So to hear that my idea of normality was everything but normal was quite shocking. I had to be honest with God and with my problems. It helped me to be honest with the people I loved."

That's when the music slowly returned, and Marisa's life took a new path. She says she started taking her faith seriously.

She got involved in summer camp and learned a lot about pouring into others, then became a camp counselor. She got involved in a youth group at her church, and she started singing for the first time in a long time when she was invited to join the worship team.

"I've always sang," she says. "Even when I was with my birth mom, I sang. I knew I always wanted to sing. I joined a band to learn to read music. I can't be myself without singing."

Above all else, Marisa wanted to sing. God had given her the gift of music, and not even the trauma would take it away. After high school she pursued a college degree in worship arts at a small university near her hometown. She trained to sing from the stage, specifically to draw others close to God. She snagged a position with a traveling worship band. That's where she met her husband, the lead vocalist.

But the past would find her in her present.

> **IT IS POSSIBLE TO UPROOT HIDDEN HURTS, PUT WORDS AND REASONS TO THEM, AND DIG DEEP FOR THE MOTIVATION TO KEEP MOVING FORWARD.**

"Four years into our relationship and two years into our marriage, I broke down," she says. "My husband knew I had days that were sad. What he didn't know was how to connect the dots. He had never dealt with depression. One evening, we were sitting outside at Starbucks. I completely broke down and told him I didn't want to live anymore. I heard the words come out of my mouth: 'I don't care whether I am here or not. I don't care if I die. I don't care how I die.' Telling him was one of the most difficult things I have ever done but also one of the best things I've ever done. Because we talked about it, I made a decision that day that I didn't want to be like this anymore. I needed to find someone to talk to, and not just my husband. That's when a lot of healing started."

It's to be expected that Marisa had a lot of reboots. But between the music and the meltdowns, she says she's growing. Over time and with help, she is learning that it is possible to uproot hidden hurts, put words and reasons to them, and dig deep for the motivation to keep moving forward. She attends mental health classes and is learning strategies to overcome the nightmares, fear, lack of self-worth, and feelings of abandonment. She believes survivors are the ones who see they can do something good for themselves. They don't wait around doing nothing.

"All these years later I am still struggling with depression. But I am not suicidal anymore. I know there will be better days and I want to be a part of those better days. I have to take care of myself in order to be a part of those beautiful days. I have a five-month-old baby girl. I want to be healthy for her. I don't want to be what my mom was. I needed to recognize there may be a chance of being like her, and I needed to face it head-on."

She pulls out her phone and shows me pictures of her baby and her husband.

"You know, you present yourself as if you have your life together," I point out.

"It's like that with anyone," she says. "I don't have it all together. Most people don't."

"You're right. All of us have something going on that others can't see. Me included."

Marisa nods. "You can't judge a book by its cover. We all have our own set of issues."

"Yes," I say. We can fool our friends and family about who we really are, but God knows what's going on inside. It is impossible to fool him, because nothing in all of creation is hidden from God's sight (Hebrews 4:13).

Marisa breathes deeply. Her confession is raw and earthy, from the ashes. "He is the Rock I stand on. It doesn't matter where I am or how I am feeling—happy or sorrowful, he is with me in both the mess and happiness. It's hard to grasp that idea when all you've known is abandonment. But he doesn't run from me. He is alongside me, in front of me, and behind me. I love that about God. It doesn't matter what you are going through. He loves you and is with you.

"I want to survive," she continues. "No. More than survive. Who's to say good things won't happen?

"I am taking care of my stuff," she continues. "My bio mom didn't. That's the difference. You can't run from issues. You have to face them. Now that I have a family, I am doing things to prevent my past trauma from affecting us. I have forgiven my bio mom, but there is still fear. I have forgiven the hurt, but I still hesitate. I have triggers that impact me, like loud voices take me back to her yelling. It is all a part of me, but I deal with it. You can move past it, or you can hold on to it, because where you go is up to you. You can choose to be a victim of your environment and what happened to you, or you can choose to move forward. Trauma doesn't have to define you."

She continues. "The path behind me isn't the one that I would have wanted for myself, but what is in front of me can be—and is—significantly better than what was. I need to give my future the opportunity to be better than my past."

I smile. "I'm struck by your resilience."

"I want to teach my daughter how to deal with life's punches. I can't guide her through a mess if I'm a mess," Marisa says.

A few weeks after we met, I logged on to Facebook and clicked on the church service link Marisa sent me. It was a recording of Marisa standing next to her husband in front of the cameras, leading virtual worship. As a little girl, she could not have imagined a life filled with song, a voice praising God, a loving husband, and a beautiful baby girl.

How does a girl who was saturated in childhood trauma sing again? By accepting the past, getting help to change the future, and singing one song at a time. That's how the music returns.

SEARCH FOR ANSWERS . . . OR NOT

IT'S NORMAL, OKAY, AND EXPECTED

Blessed is the one who perseveres under trial.

JAMES 1:12

CHAPTER 20

WHEN I WENT BACK

Life is made of ever so many partings welded together.

CHARLES DICKENS

WHAT WOULD IT be like to study abroad? Hundreds of thousand of US students do it each year. Imagine exploring castles, churches, ancient ruins, trying new foods, practicing a new language, making new friends, and becoming independent and self-sufficient. That's what Logan did.

He attended school in Shanghai, a modern city twice the size of New York rising out of ancient architecture, temples, and ruins from as early as 4000 BC. He says the university is located near all the amenities. He could walk, bike, or take public transportation to a huge shopping mall, restaurants, and movie theaters, anytime he wanted. Exciting stuff for a guy who normally attends a Midwest university that sits smack-dab in the middle of a cornfield, great for stargazing and corn mazes but not so great for a sizzling adventure. That came with Shanghai, with immersion in Mandarin, life in a dorm with Chinese roommates, and weekends on a high-speed train exploring China.

Logan is twenty-two and will soon graduate with a double major in international business and marketing. He's not only an excellent student, he's also a good-looking guy with a gentle smile.

Sixty students were in his graduating class from high school. The university he goes to is small too. China was his first big, long-term adventure away from home without his family. You might be wondering, Why China and not Greece or Spain? Logan is Chinese. He was four when an American couple adopted him. For him, it made sense to go back to where he was born.

"It was a steep learning curve at first," he says about arriving in China. "The culture is so different, and I am not very good with Chinese. Some students picked it up right away. I struggled but did better after I stuffed two semesters of Mandarin into one semester while I was there. I learned eight hundred characters while everyone else learned four hundred. It was intense," he says. "I learned fast."

Over the next three months, between classes and exploring Shanghai, he quickly made friends from all over the world, just as he had hoped. He shared a tiny dorm room with a Chinese student, rather than an American, so he could feel immersed in the experience. He hung out in the student lounge and kitchen with Chinese students and watched them fire up their woks and cook traditional foods they had eaten all their lives. They coaxed, tricked, or let's just say highly persuaded him to try the indigenous food. Once he took a pungent bite of fermented fried tofu. He could barely make sense of the taste.

"It made my eyes sting. One bite was enough," he laughs.

In a Shanghai street market, he inhaled the exotic smells and tasted unimaginable street food such as squid on a stick. He tried fried milk, a sweetened concoction, breaded, and then fried. He often passed on the unidentifiable wiggly things in water buckets, opting for his favorite slow-cooked pork and noodles. Elbow-to-elbow with people who looked like him, he says he clung to his new friends from around the world, not having a clue at first how to navigate the city.

But he didn't get homesick. With everything at his fingertips, he says, he didn't have time for it.

"I had so much fun. I didn't think about being away from home. I promised myself that I'd be spontaneous when I got to China."

His decision to study abroad was all about the adventure and school. But something deep nudged him too. He didn't think he wanted to go back to see where he was born and lived for four years. But he was so close, too close to not do it. So he set a plan in motion.

"Can you tell me about you and China and your first years?" I ask.

"Someone found me when I was about a month old," he says.

"Do you know any details?"

"I may have been abandoned because I had medical issues. I had a heart murmur. My heart couldn't pump enough blood to my body, so I would turn blue sometimes."

"That sounds pretty serious."

"My parents told me it was a miracle that I even got the heart surgery I needed back then since the orphanage was really poor."

Logan grew up in a typical home with a dad (who is a teacher), his mom, and four homegrown sisters and a brother. He grew up in a '90s walkout ranch-style house. His sisters were loud and outgoing and sang a lot. His older brother and he played all the time. He says he was spoiled at first but quickly became just another part of the gang.

Typically, kids begin feeling their separation story in their teens. Not Logan.

IT WASN'T UNTIL I WENT TO COLLEGE THAT MY CHINESE HERITAGE AND BIRTH STORY BECAME IMPORTANT. I WAS SEPARATED FROM MY PARENTS FOR THE FIRST TIME, AND IT GOT ME THINKING.

"When I was a teenager, my adoption was in the back of my head," he says. "Being adopted was something I rarely thought about or wondered about until college. It wasn't until I went to college that my Chinese heritage and birth story became important. I was separated from my parents for the first time, and it got me thinking. I also met students from China on campus. That's when I started to think more about it."

"So you were in China, goofing around, taking it all in, attending classes and studying, I imagine, and something urged you to go to where you were born? What happened next?"

"One weekend we took the high-speed train to Luoyang, the ancient capital of China. Luoyang was close to where I was adopted. We arrived, checked into our hotel, and spent the rest of the day looking around. That's when I arranged for a private guide. The next morning I went alone with him to Jiaozuo, two hours away.

"When we pulled in, it was warm and very windy. It was weird to think that this place in front of my eyes was the same place I lived almost eighteen years ago. I was surprised I didn't remember it. Everything was different."

Logan says he wandered the grounds and came upon the main building, which looked pretty nice inside. There were a lot of classrooms too.

"They not only teach the orphans, but also kids of poor families nearby. I saw they also had water therapy for kids with disabilities. Most of the kids were napping when I arrived. But I did see kids taking lessons in a few of the classrooms. Things looked newer. It may as well have been a different orphanage."

He said he stumbled over a few Chinese phrases trying to speak to the orphanage director and a worker who didn't remember him.

"I was hoping for a little bit of closure, but it didn't happen."

"How did you feel?" I ask.

"I felt dissatisfied. I didn't see the exact building where I lived after I was abandoned. I took a few pictures, but not many since it looked like a completely different place after all these years. In the end, it kind of felt like it was good to see. I still have questions—just the big ones, like why I was given up and by whom."

"But you took the risk and went there," I offer. "It sounds like you needed to go and see and experience it. Maybe in some way it helped just being there."

"I think so. Most of the memories that came from being there made me wish I could do things over, like learning Chinese at an earlier age or pushing harder to incorporate more of my heritage into my life. Plus, I wish I went back to the orphanage a lot sooner. I'm determined to go back and actually look for my biological parents."

To be in China, so close to his birthplace and not go back . . . I was glad he did. I could tell it was a bittersweet experience, but eye-opening too.

"Before I went to China, I knew I wanted to be there. After going there, I'll eventually get back there to work or study again. I am very American now, but it was so cool to see where I came from again and to actually be surrounded by people who look like me. It was different but cool. I feel excited. It confirmed everything for me. It sparked a return date."

He continues. "I remember something I read once. Today more than ever I get it. 'Your biological mother gave you the ability to love; your adopted mother gave you the ability to show love.' Both families are very important to me. I wish I would have understood this as a teen, but now I do."

CHAPTER 21

ALL-AMERICAN GUATEMALAN SOUTHERN GIRL

Curiosity: A strong desire to know or learn something or someone.

AT AGE TWENTY, standing four feet and eleven and a half inches tall—she always counts the half so she can feel a little taller—Kaylin lives with her family in the southwest corner of Louisiana near Texas, about an hour-and-a-half drive from the Gulf of Mexico. She was adopted from Guatemala as a baby and is proud of her story. Currently she's a cashier and sometimes student, living in what Louisianans call a "parish," a hand-me-down French term for a county.

Kaylin describes herself as an artist and crafter. She's also an extrovert who is really good with people. Most days you'll find her wearing jeans, a nice top, and either Converse or sandals. She has a boyfriend and a great family.

"You sound like an all-American girl," I point out.

"Yes, ma'am," she says in her upbeat southern Louisiana accent, and I smile. Being from the north, I find her lilting drawl oh-so-contagious. I have to contain myself from answering back with my own version of a Southern accent.

She describes three defining moments when she started piecing together her adoption story.

"When I was seven, I noticed for the first time I was the only olive-skinned, brown-haired kid on the playground."

In the thought life of a second grader, she figured one day she would simply dye her hair blonde to look like the rest of them.

Then somewhere between second and third grade, while playing with friends, she innocently concluded that her skin was just dirty.

"I thought if I rubbed it, it would get clean."

Of course, it didn't work. She finds it funny now.

"I don't know why I went there in my head," she laughs.

We talk about how normal it is for kids to do stuff like that to figure things out. For her, it was like an ongoing mystery she needed to solve.

"I remember learning about Martin Luther King Jr. in social studies class," she says. I saw his photo and skin color in my textbook, and I asked my mom if I was African American."

"What did she say?"

"She said I was from Guatemala."

"Did it make sense?"

"I was like, okay. I was still pretty young," she says.

Around the same time, her mom told her what she knew about Kaylin's birth family and the village near Antigua, Guatemala, where she had been born. Over the next few years, Kaylin got increasingly curious.

"I have three younger non-bio siblings who were also adopted from Guatemala, but I'm the curious one."

The summer of her freshman year of high school, she and her family traveled with their church on a mission trip to Guatemala. She was fourteen. Their small group served at an orphanage and put on a Vacation Bible School for the kids in the village.

"What was it like seeing so many kids who look like you?" I ask.

"It opened my eyes," she says. "The people are happy. They are so beautiful. They didn't appear to crave material things like we do in the States. It made me want to be like them and not be greedy or want a lot of stuff."

After that trip, she planned to return to Guatemala after graduation, this time to meet her birth family . . . if she could find them. She pulled everyone into her dream, including her boyfriend, who helped her with the research. Together they grew more and more excited. She wanted him and her family to join her when she traveled to Guatemala to meet her birth family.

"I raised the money to hire a searcher. I contacted her. I sent her pictures and a letter. I sent the money," she says proudly.

The last thing to do was to wait. Waiting was hard she explains. You don't know if they will want to meet you or if they are even alive. In less than two weeks, her wait was over. An email appeared in her inbox. Her heart pounded. She clicked on it. The searcher had found her birth mother!

"I was so happy. 'Scared happy,'" she clarifies. "I was nervous and shocked, and I didn't know what to expect."

She says a thousand questions came to mind. She quickly typed things like, "Is she alive? Does she remember me? Does she want to talk to me?" She was preparing herself for the worst. Then she held her breath.

"So she was alive?" I ask.

"Yes, ma'am," her voice lilts and brightens.

"And wanted to see you?"

"Yes, ma'am."

The rest of her family waited in suspense. When she shared the exciting news, her parents were excited but her mom gently cautioned, "Don't take it hard if your birth mother needs time to get over the shock of learning about you."

I ask her how quickly she traveled to Guatemala.

"A few months later. My mom, dad, and my boyfriend went with me."

The four arrived on a Thursday and spent a few days in Antigua shopping and touring the city—a blend of modern and Spanish-Baroque colonial architecture with cobbled streets, located at the base of an active volcano. Kaylin says they wandered the market and drifted from stall to stall looking at the fresh fish, tropical vegetables, meats, colorful homemade blankets, and handcrafted jewelry. She noticed women carried baskets of fruit on their heads.

"What happened next?"

"On Sunday, when our searcher arrived, we went to the small village in her car, only ten minutes from Antigua," she says. "I wasn't sure how the first meeting would go."

"I imagine you were nervous. I know I'd be."

"I can't describe the feeling. We pulled up to a tiny house, got out, and our translator walked to the door while we waited. I saw her come out. Then she led my birth mother to me. We stood face-to-face. Neither of us knowing what to do. I didn't know if I should hug her, or what. It was kind of awkward. We didn't know each other, but at the same time we did."

She describes the first minutes as a little more formal than she had expected.

"So you eventually hugged?"

"Yes, ma'am. It was really weird seeing her at first. All my life, I only had a small picture of her from my adoption file. She never in a million years thought I would contact her. She was in disbelief."

"What was going through your head?"

"Oh, my gosh! That's the person who gave birth to me! She's real. She's in front of me. This is where I would have grown up." She stops to think. "It was great, but at the same time . . ." She pauses again and struggles to find the right words.

I notice the confusion in her stops and starts. It was a lot to process. At last she continues.

"I guess, because I haven't known them for twenty years, and they were like strangers but also family, it's hard to explain."

The two families met in a blur of hugs. They were welcomed into the house. Soon Kaylin's biological sisters and brothers arrived, toting their babies and toddlers on their hips, and the small space filled to the brim.

"My dad hit his head on the ceiling," she recalls.

"That's a low ceiling!" I laugh.

Next, one of her sisters hugged her and handed her a baby.

"My head was spinning," she says. "I didn't expect that."

"Maybe it was her special way of saying you're a part of the family, a cultural thing?" I offer.

One by one, all the sisters gave their babies to Kaylin and

her family, and her boyfriend too. They smiled big, carried on a conversation through their translator, and switched out babies as they sat there and talked.

"We had a full house of people. We took pictures and selfies," she says.

Slowly, her birth mother shared her story.

Through the voice of her translator, Kaylin learned that her birth mother was single. She was in her midforties. At sixteen, she had her first of ten kids. She explained the six oldest siblings had one dad, her then-husband.

Kaylin adds, "Then she had me with another man."

She pauses to take a breath.

"She knew I wouldn't be accepted by the village community because the affair was taboo."

"So she was protecting you?" I offer.

"Yes."

"And the younger three?"

"I didn't ask," she says.

"She says she gave me up for a better life. I had always thought that. I am so beyond grateful that she wanted this for me. My whole family is so grateful too, that we are together."

After meeting her biological family, Kaylin felt some sense of closure. Things that didn't make sense while growing up now do. She says she now knows more of who she is.

> **NOW I HAVE ANSWERS. IT IS BEAUTIFUL TO BE GUATEMALAN.**

"I always wondered why I love crafting, art, sewing, crocheting, and cooking."

She believes her talents and interests were passed on to her from her Guatemalan ancestors.

"Now I have answers. It is beautiful to be Guatemalan."

Recently, she stayed in Antigua for a month with a Spanish immersion program. She was able to visit her family while there, and she talks with them often.

"We message through WhatsApp or Messenger. It doesn't feel like we are strangers anymore."

Being curious about your birth family is normal. Of course, anyone who searches has to be prepared for any outcome— sometimes you can't find a birth family, or they don't want to or know how to have a relationship with you, or your adoptive family might be hesitant. If you are ready, you do you. And like Kaylin did, include your family. If you find yourself at the end of your search and you have no information, you followed your heart and gave yourself the gift of trying. You are not alone.

One of the things you might try is taking a DNA test. It won't give you the names of your birth parents, but it is something to see the cluster of dots—aka your cousins—sparkle brightly all over the map.

CHAPTER 22

WHY THEM AND NOT ME?

God will make a way.

PARAPHRASE OF ISAIAH 43:16

MEGAN WAS ADOPTED from Hefei Anhui, China, at eight months old. The orphanage director told her parents that she was found outside a police station and placed in a foster family for a few months. "Who knows," Megan says. "I might have been strapped to the back of my foster mother, working the fields."

Megan and I first met via email, then phone calls, and finally on FaceTime. She's a funny, fun-loving young woman who's content to hang out in a hammock by the lake with a bag of chips.

I quickly find out Megan is a Michigan State University psychology grad, a Spartan who grew up watching University of Michigan Wolverine football with her Wolverine-smitten, sweatshirt-wearing family. It sounds like her parents don't hold it against her until game day.

At twenty-four, she is interning as a school psychologist at the high school one town over. She invites teens into her office to help them navigate stuff in their world. Helping kids figure things out is her passion. She loves her job and loves the kids.

And from what I can tell, she's just a big kid herself. I spot her wearing a fresh coat of bird's-egg-blue nail polish and call her on it. She smiles big and wiggles her fingers in front of the camera. "My mom gave it to me in my stocking for Christmas. It's from the movie *Frozen*." We both laugh, which breaks the ice (pun intended), and as we relax into her story, Megan slouches comfortably on her couch in sweats, surrounded by blankets.

"I've lived in Florida, Connecticut, Hong Kong, and Michigan," she says.

"Wait," I interject. "Why did you move around so much? And Hong Kong? How did you end up in Hong Kong? That's so cool."

"My dad was a pastor. We moved a lot. We went to Hong Kong when he got a job at an international church on Lantau Island, a twenty-minute ferry ride from mainland Hong Kong."

Megan says she was ten when she, her mom, her dad, and her younger sister moved to Hong Kong from Connecticut for three years. They lived in a third-floor, three-bedroom apartment on Lantau Island, where people either took a bus or drove golf carts instead of cars to get around. Wide-eyed in a tropical setting, surrounded by water with the mainland within reach, she simply adored living there.

During the school week, Megan and her sister attended a British international school. Each morning they'd pull on their uniforms, gather with groups of other uniformed kids at street level, take a bus to the dock, grab seats on a high-speed ferry, take a twenty-minute ride across the crystal-blue water to the mainland, and then take another bus to the school. "You knew who went to which school based on the uniforms," she says.

She loved testing her wings in the megacity.

"You were what ten, eleven, twelve?"

I tell her that seems a tad young for "free range" in a mega-city. She laughs.

"Hong Kong was so safe. I could jump in a red taxi or subway and meet my friends at the mall or go to my friend's apartment by myself," she says.

There was a lot to love about Hong Kong: Hi-Chew candy, an intense, chewy fruit candy similar to Starburst. The crunch of Mamee, her favorite dry noodle snack, something like ramen with salty seasoning that's almost like eating a bag of chips, Hong Kong–style. Chinese New Year (in February, by the way). Dragon Boat Festival. Fireworks on a hot summer night. International foods of every kind. She misses all of it.

"You may think I was searching for myself in Hong Kong or wanting to know myself as a young Chinese girl. Truth is, it was just me having fun. I was too young to process any of that yet."

Megan always knew why she was adopted. She was given up because her family was forced to comply with the One Child Policy,[1] strictly enforced by authorities to counter population growth in China.

"Knowing this gave me a better understanding of my situation. Without that background information, it would be easier to judge my birth parents. In a way, knowing why [they gave me up] created more empathy in me."

In addition, Megan was told her birth family most likely lived in the countryside. Were they farmers? Herders? She doesn't know the specifics. Either way, rural Chinese families depend on crops for food and income. Sons work the land and, according to tradition, are more valued than daughters for that reason. Sons are also expected to care for their parents in their old age, like an insurance policy.

"My parents never hid the facts of why I was adopted," Megan says. "The *why* made sense, sort of. They also always told me that God placed me in their arms, and he knew the plans for me."

Megan never had any reason to doubt what she was told. Nothing was kept from her. Sketchy details were based on highly rational assumptions. On top of that, her childhood was filled with every opportunity to explore her Chinese heritage—celebrating her adoption day each year, hosting international exchange students from China, and taking classes in Chinese, all of which she is so thankful for. Yet something still bothered her. She still wondered if she knew the total true story. She got her chance to find out at the sprawling campus of Michigan State University, located in the center of Michigan's mitten.

"I was a freshman at MSU. Second semester, I got a new roommate. She was from China! I also began meeting other international students from China around campus. It got me thinking—they were my age, eighteen, and they were girls. How could that be? Why weren't they given up too? Why did their parents keep them? What's their story? Why was I relinquished when others were not? What did their families believe or have that was different from my birth family? I just wanted to hear it from them."

Megan had a bunch of questions I found fascinating. She started out by observing these Chinese girls who looked like her. But it was knowing they had real families back in China that made Megan question what was going on. It occupied her thoughts on and off from one semester to the next. She couldn't help herself. She had to hear why they had their first family and she didn't.

That winter of her freshman year, after making friends with

more Chinese international students on campus, Megan got her chance. One in particular became her closest friend. They became so close that Megan felt comfortable enough to ask her all the questions she'd been holding inside.

"My friend was an only child and a girl. So one night in the dorm, it was just the two of us. I don't remember what exactly we were doing, but we were just casually talking about China. I asked her where she was from, and she told me she grew up in Taizhou, in Zhejiang province, a big city on the China Sea coast. She also told me her parents were business owners, and they ran a paper company."

"Okay." I nod. "That's interesting. She's a city girl. Then what did you ask?"

"I bluntly asked her—did your parents prefer boys to girls?"

"That's direct and honest," I say. "So you were trying to get a read on if there was any sort of partiality? What did she say?"

"She said no. Her parents did not prefer boys over girls, and boys and girls were viewed equally."

"What were you thinking at that moment?"

"At first, I was frustrated. I couldn't understand why her parents hadn't given her up for adoption. It was so confusing. Suddenly the *why* of my story no longer made sense."

Megan's mind kept trailing back to what she'd been told her whole life. Girls were often relinquished, boys were more valued. Seeing loads of Chinese girls on campus only confirmed what her friend had told her that night. There were girls in China, apparently a lot, who were raised by their biological parents. And it turned out many had the financial means to send them to college in the States too. It seemed to Megan that the One Child Policy wasn't a fear or worry for people with means.

"It sounds to me like this was all very eye-opening. Were you bothered by what you learned?" I ask.

"No," Megan replies. "I was just trying to sort it all out. I just didn't know—why me? Now I get it. Their families were in a different situation than mine. They were well-off. They had the resources a rural family doesn't have. Urban or rural, if you don't have the resources, you don't have choices."

"So did it help to talk it through with your friend?"

"Yes. I needed that proof, for some reason, to fully accept the story I was told. I needed the validation. I needed the truth. I needed closure. I've accepted my story because there's nothing my birth family could have done."

She continues on another thought.

> " GOD WAS PROTECTING ME AND WRITING MY STORY, AND THAT GIVES ME COMFORT.

"I am grateful I am not just a statistic. The Chinese government has so much power, but ultimately God has control. God was protecting me and writing my story, and that gives me comfort. He knew how all of this was going to play out. My parents always told me God had plans for my life. I believe he does, and it gives me peace. I believe God made a way for me. It might have been harder for me to accept being given up if I didn't have God's love and acceptance of me in my heart."

Megan has advice for anyone in a similar situation.

"When you get to college, you'll meet people who look like you with a different story from yours. You may have questions, like I did. It is okay to ask. Please do. Ask away. It is an amazing way to figure things out."

I imagine Megan moving around campus watching people, thinking about her own story while imagining theirs. Then she has a closure moment with her roommate. Maybe her story will help you accept your story too. The thing is, if Megan never finds out anything about her birth family, never knows, she believes that no matter why you or she were separated from your birth families, the Author of Life intervenes again and again. Like Megan says, he is not absent. He has the pen in his hands and a plan for you.

CHAPTER 23

SOMETHING SPECIAL ABOUT KATE

Never forget where you've been. Never lose sight of where you're going. And never take for granted the people who travel the journey with you.

SUSAN GALE WICKES

In the middle of June 2019, Kate, then eighteen, her parents, and her fifteen-year-old brother—who, like Kate, was born in Russia—made the trip to St. Petersburg to be reunited with several members of her birth family. Kate's adoptive family arrived on a perfect day in the most opulent, westernized city in all of Russia. Kate, a petite, five-foot-one blonde, says she stood on her tippy-toes near the luggage carousel, heart racing, searching the crowd while her parents and brother hauled their suitcases off the belt. Their overnight flight had begun in Detroit, stopped in Philly, then landed in London that morning with one more leg to go. Traveling has its challenges; Kate says they almost missed their Aeroflot flight to St. Petersburg. Nothing like adding a little more tension to an already intense experience. When the landing gear connected with the tarmac at Pulkovo Airport outside St. Petersburg, the family of four gave a collective sigh of relief.

"To have my Russian family think we were going to show up and then us not . . . I panicked in London. I couldn't breathe and couldn't stop crying. It was a miracle they held the plane for us."

Born in March 2001, Katarina was the fourth daughter of her single mom, who lived near Arkhangelsk—a large city known for harvesting timber from endless forests for construction, and a three-hour flight north of St. Petersburg. When Kate was born, her birth mother was struggling, and, at the time of Kate's visit, still did. So Kate wasn't sure she'd be reuniting with her birth mother, but she was positive she would be meeting other members of her family, and one in particular: her oldest sister, Natasha.

Natasha, who was fifteen when Kate was born, grew up watching her mom struggle and stumble from one day to the next. When her mom got pregnant with her fourth baby, the situation became dire. Their mother had been unstable financially and hadn't worked in years. The two were living on a government stipend, a small amount of rubles for food and necessities and a small apartment. Her two younger sisters had been sent to live with their maternal grandmother; no dad, husband, nor grandfather was around to lend a hand. But Natasha was old enough to understand. She could read the Cyrilic writing on the wall. What would happen to *this* new baby when she was born? Would she go to babushka too, or worse, would Natasha lose her forever?

Natasha took matters into her own hands.

Over the weeks leading up to Kate's birth, Natasha planned. She was determined she would take care of the new baby, even if she had to miss school. She was smart and resourceful; she'd catch up. The baby was too important. When Kate was born, Natasha helped as much as she could. But her mother was overwhelmed, to say it nicely, and ultimately unable to care for her newborn. One day, she bundled up Kate and took a bus to the baby home. It was not uncommon for struggling parents to use the baby home when life's punches got too rough. She could always return for her baby. She hadn't signed away her parental rights.

Natasha begged her mother before she left not to do it. *Please, please, I'll do everything. You won't have to do anything.* She promised to give up school, friends, even sleep to take care of Kate. Finally, after a month, her mother agreed, and Kate came home. Natasha could breathe again. Night feedings, rocking, diaper changes, laundry, and attending classes filled her days and nights. She poured every ounce of herself into caring for her infant sister. There was something about Kate. She just couldn't let her go. Meanwhile, she was missing too much school. It was her senior year, and the school administrator had noticed. School is compulsory in Russia, and rules are rules. So the police checked in, reported the situation to the court, and, as Kate tells me, "I was ripped from my home and taken back to the baby home." Her sister had held on to her for a year.

Kate says her birth mother eventually signed away her parental rights so Kate could be adopted. Weeping, Natasha was devastated when she said goodbye. By now Kate had been crawling and getting ready to walk. Little did the two sisters know they would be bonded for life; an attachment had formed that would last forever.

"At that time, my birth mother was a heavy drinker, I'm told," Kate says. "I'm not exactly sure of the whole situation. It was my sister who showed me how much she really loved me and cared for me."

I offer, "I'm convinced tiny babies bond and make connections. You were smart, alert, and aware of what was going on. And even though you didn't have the words, it appears you never forgot Natasha's choice to put you first."

"I loved her and still love her. She was the person who took care of me since my birth when our mother wasn't able to."

In the orphanage, Kate looked for Natasha's familiar smile and listened for her soothing voice but was soon swallowed up in a crowd of hungry mouths and busy toddlers. By the time Kate was almost three, her profile, along with others, was posted on a data bank of kids available for adoption from Arkhangelsk. That's when her adoptive parents saw her picture and were immediately drawn to her. And the connection was real, her mom says, sitting next to Kate and sharing the memory. From first sight, they knew Kate was their daughter. Other crazy things added up too, such as their long, drawn-out, multisyllabic Russian last name. The couple had Russian roots! It turns out her dad's great-grandfather, Mikhail, had immigrated with his family from the Soviet Union as a kid.

In November 2003, Tammy and Chris flew to Russia to adopt Kate. Three years later, they returned to Arkhangelsk to adopt a son. The family of four was complete, sort of. Kate's mom wasted no time in beginning to search for the kids' birth families. She says she knew that these people were an important part of their story.

Then in 2006, when Kate was just six, Tammy hired a searcher to find Kate's birth mother. She figured it would get more difficult to discover information later if she waited. In an unexpected twist, the searcher not only found Kate's birth mother, who at first was startled by his visit yet receptive, but she then pointed him to Natasha. Now twenty, Natasha stood face-to-face with the searcher and relayed her story, tears streaming down her cheeks in a wash of relief. As she swiped away the dampness, she couldn't believe it. Five years had elapsed. Her sister was in the US. She never expected to hear from her or see her gain. And now she was being offered a second chance.

She took it. And over the next fourteen years, letters and photos crossed the ocean as the two girls kept in touch. In spite of the hit-or-miss efforts of the Russian mail system, both sisters got everything they sent the other. Two photo albums slowly took shape.

"You said you had a unique connection to your sister," I say. "Your mom obviously believed in the connection too."

"Yes, my mom was very open with me about my birth family. I am very grateful. Some people are afraid."

Enter Russian VK a few years later, a popular website something like the Russian version of Facebook. In 2018, Kate and her mom downloaded Russian VK. They were like two giddy little kids. They used Google Translate to communicate with Kate's birth family for the first time online.

"After fourteen years, we were able to finally communicate face-to-face!" Kate says. "Through all the communication over months, we decided to go visit my three sisters. We renewed all the passports, a huge, ugly process. Then filled out tons of paperwork. Finally we applied for visas. We purchased plane tickets for us and them, being considerate of their financial situation. My mom connected with a friend in St. Petersburg to translate."

The date was set.

Back at the luggage carousel, in a burst of joy, Kate spotted Natasha and her kids in the crowd and waved first.

"They ran to me and gave me a big hug," she says.

The synchronized arrival plan had worked. With luggage in tow, the small group collected outside the doors and found their translator hovering by the exit. Over the next five days, Kate says, the sisters shared a lifetime of missed moments, comparing similarities, asking questions, and making new memories.

Kate wore her backpack from the plane, filled with carefully selected gifts for each of her family members. Eyes adjusting to the bright sunlight, the group hugged again and held on while their emotions settled. Through the translator, everyone got acquainted.

"Your birth mother couldn't come?" I ask.

"No," Kate says. "I didn't get to meet my mom face-to-face, but I did FaceTime with her while we were there. It was okay."

There was a sense of disappointment in her voice.

"Was Natasha as wonderful as her story seemed way back then?" I ask.

"Yes, she was as compassionate and caring as she was back then. Once we unpacked our luggage, we went to a restaurant and had dinner all together. For five days we went on tours of churches, palaces, and parks and talked and ate. The ice cream is the best in Russia."

The family also ate borscht, a traditional soup with chunks of beets and beef with carrots, sauerkraut, and beef broth. Kate says it is one of her favorite foods ever.

"On the last day in St. Petersburg, we had a great big dinner with the whole family—Natasha's family plus my other two sisters, their two husbands, five nieces, two nephews, and some cousins—and after dinner we went on a nighttime river boat tour. I felt really happy. I felt complete. I didn't want the five days to end. I knew they loved me."

On the last night, they said their goodbyes, and their friend and translator dropped them back at her large two-bedroom apartment. Kate and her mom remember the space well: how the floor-to-ceiling windows brought in a cool breeze, how the tree branches filled with little white flowers reached into the windows, and how the peaceful, comforting songs of birds floated through the rooms. I think to myself, if the vintage wood parquet floors could talk, they'd have something more to talk about then the secrets of the Soviet past.

One by one, they all claimed their beds, exhausted.

"Your parents did this for you. How do you feel?" I ask.

"I feel loved," Kate smiles. "My parents trusted the process of being truthful with me from the beginning. My family in Russia is happy for me and loves me and knows I am well taken care of," she says.

"Nothing like seeing it with your own eyes."

"Some of my high school girlfriends are from Russia too. There's a bunch of us. Most of my friends don't know their birth families; they only know they were adopted. It's not a bad thing to know about your past. Talking with your birth family is perfectly okay as long as the process is done in a safe manner."

> **IT HELPS TO THINK THROUGH ALL THE PROS AND CONS OF MEETING YOUR BIRTH FAMILY.**

Kate's mom adds that it helps to think through all the pros and cons of meeting your birth family. Here is Kate and her mom's advice if you want to find your birth family and ultimately travel to meet them.

Step 1: Open the line of communication with your adoptive parents first. Tell your parents how you feel. It's okay to have questions. Trust that your parents are strong enough to answer your questions in an honest way. The less communication, the less ready you are for a reunion. Be patient with your parents; it is emotional for them too. Be mature and rational. The more you can be honest and nonemotional (not screaming, "You are not my mother!"), the better. Say, "I feel like I need to know more." It is your parents' job to make sure you know who you are.

Step 2: Start the process with a reliable third-party searcher. There's minimal risk this way. Work with the third-party intermediary until you are sure the connection is healthy on both sides. Gathering information is a part of the process, but it should be gathered safely. Don't just jump on VK or any other Facebook site and message unknown people. Do it responsibly through a searcher. Why? There could be five hundred people with the same name; the last thing you want to do is send a message to the wrong person or someone who doesn't want to be found.

Step 3: Once you have the information, your parents should assess it. Children tend to react emotionally. Parents can be more objective. Remember that there were circumstances leading up to the fact that you were given a different forever family. Getting information could take months. The search could stop with just pictures and information. If there is enough information, and it is enough for you, let it be enough. But feel free to pursue it later if you'd like. It's okay to take breaks. Kate's mom says, "We never pushed our kids to pursue a relationship with their birth families.

It is something that evolved over a long period of time—fourteen years!" Sometimes it is wise to end the pursuit for contact if the relationship will not produce a healthy and happy outcome. It's also important to hold expectations loosely and brace yourself for another rejection.

Step 4: Whether you travel or not should be your choice. If you don't want to continue to have a conversation or relationship and even travel, let your parents know. Kids have fantasies about how amazing your reunion could be, but your adoptive parents have the backstory. You have to trust that your parents will guide you well—they witnessed your life in another place with their own eyes. If they are open to discussing this life with you, trust that they will guide you in the right direction. You want to have a reunion in a safe, trusting environment. You overcame so much transitioning from one country and one family to another. It would be devastating to enter a relationship that would set your progress backward. Kate's mom says, "We had years of dialogue on both sides before we traveled—allowing a trusting relationship to form between all family members."

Step 5: Wait until you are mentally prepared to hold the experience in your heart in a healthy way. The longer you can wait the better able you will be to embrace the fullness of the experience.

CHAPTER 24

I JUST WANT TO SEE

I had another family . . .

SAROO BRIERLEY

NOT ALL BIRTH family reunions go as planned. Take Alek's story. He just wanted to meet his birth mother, see who he came from, and piece together why he looks like, well, himself. He had his chance when he was fifteen. He was steps away, literally, from meeting his birth mother, but things didn't go as hoped. He tells me he wants a second chance, that if she doesn't want to meet him, well, tough. He just wants to see.

Born Aleksei Dmitrievich in Nizhny Novgorod, Russia, and adopted as a toddler, Alek—with a K not an X—rolls his name off his tongue like a native Russian. The precise pronunciation gives me a glimpse of his growing pride in his heritage and a subtle hint that being born in Russia still matters to him. It's a part of his story, a piece of him that will never change. Why not embrace it? But it took him time to come to this conclusion. Mostly because he wanted to forget, move on, be American, be a typical teen. He didn't need more. As he puts it, "I am Americanized."

Now twenty-two, Alek works for a small tool-and-die shop in Michigan and says he loves it. He works there while also working on his associate's degree in business at the local community college. He quickly admits he has ADHD, as if to set the record straight, but he didn't let that derail him, and he didn't call it quits when school got hard. School has never been easy, he says. But he's a worker, and he makes things happen. Today, besides programming, he runs a mechanical high-power water pressure wand, a cutting tool so intense it can cut steel into automotive parts. It's fun. It's creative. It keeps him on his toes, and he likes that.

It's early Sunday afternoon, Alek's day off, when I pull into his driveway. I check out the '70s style white ranch nestled into the woods, a recent purchase. Alek, slim frame and dark brown hair, waits at the front door and waves me in. We are meeting for the first time, and this interview "thing" is a first for him. A football game plays on the big flat-screen TV mounted on a shiplap wall, the focal point of the room. I tuck my half boots on the rug to the right, just inside the door. Alek introduces me to his roommate, who says hi and politely makes himself scarce. "Do you want some coffee?" Alek offers, his emerald-green eyes sparkling with mischief. "I don't know how to greet people yet," he admits with a laugh. It has only been two months since he bought the place.

I reassure him he's being the perfect host, and I ooh and ah over his tidy place, which is an unexpected surprise. No stinky pile of clothes in the corner. No leftover Chinese takeout on the counter. The fresh, white kitchen; the shiplap, soft gray walls; the warm brown, wood-vinyl plank floor; and the open concept remind me of the big reveal in an HGTV *Fixer Upper* episode. I take it all in as he directs me to the round oak kitchen table, where we can sit and talk. I'm thinking, this guy is set. He assures me he's worked hard. I can tell.

With a lighthearted vibe, Alek tells me he keeps busy playing a variety of sports and working out with friends—that is, when he's not working on his house or in the tool-and-die shop.

Our conversation is light and focuses on lifting weights for a while. He doesn't look like a bodybuilder type; he's lanky, not buff.

"So do you have six-pack abs?" I laugh joining in on his mischief.

He doesn't hesitate. "I wouldn't say I have them now. Maybe when I was younger."

"Seriously, can I print that?"

"Yeah. LOL."

Alek cracks me up. He's easy to talk with. He's an open book.

"How do your friends describe you?" I ask.

"They say I am goofy, funny, always busy, a project dude."

He's also a loyal fan of the Michigan teams—Detroit Lions, Pistons, and U of M.

"I like watching the players even when they're not winning," he laughs, pointing out that the Michigan teams are mostly losers at the moment.

I laugh too. "That's generous of you."

We turn to talking about Alek's birth family reunion trip. Seven years earlier he and his older adopted brother—with the help of their mom—arranged to visit Nizhny Novgorod, Russia, where both the boys were born. Nizhny, as the locals call it, was once a Soviet Union weapons town until the Soviet Union collapsed in 1991. Now it's a thriving city open to visitors.

After securing passports for the boys, visas to enter Russia, a translator, and accommodations, the two teens and their mom boarded a plane in late December for the ten-hour flight to blustery Moscow. There they met Alek's older brother's birth family first. They would attempt to meet Alek's birth mother in Nizhny later in the week.

"What was it like when you got to Moscow?" I ask.

"It was cool to see. It was weird when everyone spoke a different language."

I laugh. "I've been to Russia five times. The people I met were kind and generous, but the language barrier was tough. What else do you remember?"

"I remember Red Square and an ice-skating park set up outside a large department store."

"I have great memories of Red Square too. You know, they celebrate Christmas on January 7th over there. You were right in the middle of the celebration."

"Yeah." He smiles and leans back in his chair, eyes shifting as if searching for more trip details.

Alek admits the fine details of his trip are a blur; after all, it's been more than a few years. But he remembers being picked up at the airport in Moscow by his brother's birth family. The two families had been in touch via Facebook for months, planning and arranging. After a tearful reunion, they piled into a large rented van, spent the night in a Moscow hotel, and then drove the next day to Nizhny, some 250 miles away.

"I remember their apartment in Nizhny. It was tiny," he says, "maybe five hundred square feet. It had one bedroom, a living room–kitchen combination, and one bathroom. How they all lived in such a tiny space is messed up." He continues, "We stayed at an apartment they rented for us. Ours was larger than theirs, so they came over for dinner and spent a lot of time with us."

Alek, not sure what to expect from his brother's relations, says he was impressed by the outpouring of love.

He brightens at the memory of family meals, eating fried eggs because he was picky, and a trip to McDonald's for a taste of home. His face sours at the thought of borscht, a traditional Russian beet soup that was served too often, in his opinion. As if betraying a national secret, or his heritage, or something, he confides, "Borscht is nasty." We laugh. I agree.

I ask, "So what was it like hanging out with your brother's birth family?"

"The family was very welcoming and friendly." His face lights up. "They love sports. They're big into soccer. While we were there, Nizhny held a parade for the Olympic torch that came through town for the 2014 Sochi Olympics."

"I kind of remember the Sochi Olympics," I say.

We rehash a little soccer history. Then he tells me, "One of my brother's cousins keeps in touch with us and tries to visit each year."

"No way. That's so cool."

"Yeah."

What seemed like a perfect reunion for his brother worked out differently for Alek. It was his turn to meet his birth mother. I notice a slight tension darkening his otherwise good-natured features as he relays the story.

He and his mom were standing at street level in the cold outside his birth mother's apartment building, cars racing by. He remembers the concrete, eight-story building. Hoping for the best, not wanting to intimidate his birth mother, Alek, his mom, and their translator stood at the curb near the car, waiting, huddled in their winter gear, while his brother's birth mother went inside. They figured she had the best chance of explaining the situation and convincing her to meet Alek. Everyone thought she wouldn't refuse a meeting, knowing he was standing on the street below her apartment window in plain sight.

"I remember vividly when my brother's birth mother went up to meet her," he says. He thought he saw the window curtain slowly open and then quickly close. It didn't take long before his brother's birth mother returned and met them on the street.

"What did she say?" I ask.

"She said my birth mother didn't want to meet me."

I'm puzzled. "Just like that?"

"Yeah, something like that. I don't remember. We drove off," he says, his voice perturbed.

"I'm sorry." I imagine the slush-filled sidewalk, his mother comforting him with soothing, reassuring words.

He races to move on. I sense a mix of tension and sadness.

"I just wanted to see her," he quietly pleads.

"I know." I shake my head. "It had to be hard making sense of it at fifteen."

"Yes. But I understand now," he says. "She must have felt embarrassed. She gave someone up."

"It's possible," I say. At twenty-two, it appears Alek can empathize now, something he couldn't possibly do at fifteen.

"I'm not mad at her. The biggest problem is that I wasn't invited to go up the stairs to see her. I wanted to know why I look like this." He gestures with his hands to his face.

We further speculate about the why. Was she startled? Caught off guard? Overwhelmed and ashamed to meet a son she thought she would never see again? No matter the reason, Alek was very quiet that night when they returned to the apartment. Hurt and confused, he hid his feelings, acted like he didn't care, and buried his emotions and moved on. Or so he thought. Seven years later, he still has a tender spot in his heart for wanting to know and see his birth mother. He still wonders why he didn't get invited to climb the stairs to her apartment and see. He was steps away from meeting her.

"That's my only regret," he goes on. "I was too young. If it were today, I would have gone up. What could they do, punch me?" he says, joking to hide his frustration. "I just wanted to see." He looks at me with a sense of helplessness.

"You were so close."

"Yeah. At the time, I thought this was stupid. I shut down. I thought, 'It is what it is. I can't do anything about it.' In college, I acted like it didn't happen. I was like that for a long time. Now I am revisiting it. I'm a little smarter now than back then."

"You could go back!" I blurt out. "Or hire a searcher. Wait! You already know people there. What about your brother's cousin?"

"Yeah. He lives in Moscow."

"He could arrange it," I encourage. "Gather some pictures, WhatsApp them to him, then ask him to climb those stairs for you and deliver them and get a picture of her for you."

"I could. Yeah . . ." His voice trails off while he's thinking and nodding his head. Then he tells me, "I'd like to know if I have siblings. I'd like to get in touch with them."

We sit for a moment. I'm thinking this guy is super nice. Why didn't things turn out differently? Then randomly I ask, "Can I take your picture?"

"Sure," he says, game to pose.

"I want to remember you," I say, positioning my iPhone to snap a shot. "I want to remember what an encouragement you are to me and everyone who will read your story."

I didn't have the right words for it at that moment, but it

came to me after we parted ways that I was moved by how Alek didn't let life's blows take hold of him. Instead, he took hold of life. That's the takeaway. That's what matters.

"I know who I am," Alek says. "I am always happy. I am a goofy dude. I think I am nice." He laughs, regrouping from our journey into the past. "It took a while, but I have things figured out. I am always trying to learn stuff. If I don't know, I'll ask."

> **IF YOU DON'T WANT TO MEET YOUR BIRTH PARENTS, IT'S OKAY. IT'S YOUR CHOICE.**

"What do you want to tell anyone who is considering a reunion?" I ask. "It can go either way."

Alek thinks for a moment, then says, "If you don't want to meet your birth parents, it's okay. It's your choice. Do what's best for you that keeps you mentally stable. I live by that. Don't let other people press you into doing what you don't want to do. If you want to meet them, go for it. And if you do, you don't have to choose between families either. Learn to love both families. I'm happy. I have a great family. A great mom and dad.

"For me, seeing will be enough."

Alek may never see his birth mother, which makes him sad. But he's found happiness and purpose in spite of discouragement. Every reunion story is personal; no two are alike. Alek and his brother experienced two different outcomes. Kate too. Logan wandered the grounds of his orphanage in China looking for answers. He didn't find any. Still, all of them accept that loss is a part of their story, but their story is more than the sum of their loss. It's a mindset, a way to look at things differently. It's not always easy, but it's a place to begin.

CHAPTER 25

THE FUTURE IS WORTH FIGHTING FOR

You face your fear because the goal demands it.

ALEX HONNOLD

ISIKAH REMEMBERS THE day he thought his dreams were dead. He was fifteen years old and sprawled belly first on the bed, chest heaving, eyes squeezed shut, draining every last tear and every ounce of energy he had left. "What do I do? What do I do?" he recalls mumbling. He says the dark room covered him like a damp blanket. It gave no comfort. No one came to comfort him. Good! He had locked the door anyway. He was giving up. He begged God to do something.

Isikah, now thirty, grew up with his mom and sisters and brothers in a small wood-plank house with dirt floors in a remote village near Nairobi, the largest city in Kenya. Most villagers do not experience the modern amenities of Nairobi. People in his village live day to day and earn a minimum wage based on their skill and government guidelines. It's often below $1,000 USD per year—even less for single families without the support of a dad.

"I never knew my dad. My mom worked on a nearby farm. We didn't have a lot of money [a gentleman's way of saying they were poor]. As little kids we walked behind our mom in the fields, planting seeds or harvesting corn or weeding. I couldn't go to school consistently—I had to sacrifice and work so we could eat."

I meet Isikah at a Starbucks near his apartment. He arrives after work just ahead of me and is sitting at a two-person table talking on his cell phone. I push through the entry door, pound the snow off my boots, and we make eye contact. He quickly finishes his call, stands to shake my hand, and introduces himself in a deep Nairobi accent. His English is flawless but formal, no slang. He is my height, maybe five foot seven, solid but slim. When our hands touch, I feel an overwhelming sense of peace shift from him to me. He's come a long way, lived several lives like a cat. He's oceans away from home.

We sit down at the table together. "So are you David or Isikah?" I ask, noticing both names in the right corner of his Columbia fleece pullover.

"David at my job." He points to his computer. "Isikah to me," he says, his voice is quiet, and I lean in to hear.

"Tell me about Isikah," I ask.

He begins to tell me he is a mechanical engineer working at an automotive manufacturer.

"No," I say, "tell me about young Isikah in Kenya." In my head I already know who he is before we even meet. He's a Mully kid, taken in by the largest family in the world, the Mully Children's Family. And every Mully kid is a miracle with a remarkable story.[2]

"In Kenya, people pay to go to school," he says. "It is different than in the US."

With rarely any extra income, Isikah was like the other village kids. He attended school sporadically, with dirty feet on dirt floors. He loved being there, playing with friends and learning to read and write. But rice and corn were more important than pencils and paper.

"I fell behind working in the fields. I dreamt of school. I wanted to keep going, but I didn't know how to make it happen. How could I? I was just a kid."

So he worked, and by the time he was fifteen he had reached grade eight. He was behind. That's when his rich uncle, the one who could afford food and kerosene, decided to pay for grade eight tuition.

"If kids reach grade eight, they get sorted. If you pass the national exam, you go to high school. If you don't pass, you either pay again to repeat the classes or you go to trade school."

Grade eight was a deal breaker. Poor grades could send you somewhere you didn't want to go. Isikah's goal was high school. He needed to pass grade eight and the national exam.

"Did you pass?"

"After a lot of hard studying, I passed the national exam," he says humbly.

He earned the second highest score in his school district. The village was all abuzz. Everyone was talking about Isikah. He could go to high school! This kid was going to be someone. Everything looked hopeful until the money from his uncle dried up. Isikah's mom couldn't scrape up the tuition. His dream of going to high school was gone.

"I remember locking myself in the house and crying on my bed. I was so desperate. I had worked so hard, and I still could not go to school. I prayed, 'God, you can hear me. I want to go to school!'"

"You were losing hope?"

"I was losing hope, yes."

Days dragged. He worked, planting corn seed in a daze of hopelessness. Little did he know that, behind the scenes, his village pastor had contacted a man, Charles Mully, who might be able to help.

"I didn't know this man Mully, but he wanted to help me. I thought, *God heard my prayer!* Then I got scared when I learned Mully rescues street kids."

The more he thought about Mully's help, leaving home, living at the Mully compound, the more scared he got. At first his instincts said no.

"I could only imagine a place packed with abandoned street kids. The only thing I knew about street kids was that they were known to be violent bullies."

He was afraid. "They were going to beat me up. But I didn't have another option. If I wanted to finish high school, I had to go. Mully had a school. I had to leave my mom and brothers and sisters and everything I knew behind if I wanted to finish school."

Weighing the pros and cons, he chose to get beat up. On a hot, dusty summer day, he stood next to his mom one last time, holding his mostly empty suitcase.

"Our goodbye was short. I think we were both trying to be brave," he says.

I can't help but think how much courage it takes to believe in himself so much that he'd make such a tough decision.

"My pastor drove. I watched out the window. My village disappeared. An hour later, we pulled up to the gate to the compound."

"Sounds scary."

He says he was trembling. He was ready to face his beating, his suitcase clutched to his chest like a piece of armor.

"What was it like when you stepped inside the gate?"

"It was the most amazing thing I had ever seen."

"What? You expected a compound full of dangerous kids," I remind him.

"Yes. But my eyes saw row after row of greenhouses full of plants. Children were playing. Trees were everywhere. There were orchards and ponds. I had never seen anything like this environment or these buildings before. I didn't expect this."

It was the opposite of his old school with dirt floors and no windows. It was the opposite of everything he knew back home.

"I was greeted by the impossible! Kids came and welcomed me to their home."

And the opposite of what he had feared.

"Kids of all ages patted me on the back and walked with me, taking my empty suitcase and showing me where I could put it. I remember their big smiles and their faces so friendly. This place was something special. I could feel love from everybody. It surprised me. Looking back, being loved like that changes you. If you had a heart of stone, it was changed there."

The Mully family is the largest family in the world, made up of rescued street children including infants, toddlers, elementary-age kids, and teens plucked from the trash heaps and from under boxes or the railroad bridges of Nairobi, many by Charles Mully, a former street kid himself.

"Did Mr. Mully greet you?"

"Yes. I expected to meet a really big guy."

"Was he?"

"No. Mr. Mully was a regular guy surrounded by kids, and they were singing."

"Singing?" I smile.

"And they were calling him Daddy. It was beautiful. For the first time in my life, I got to call someone Daddy too. Having a new daddy meant a lot to me. I had missed this my whole life. When Daddy and Mama Mully took me in, I became their kid, just like all the other kids. I joined the biggest family in the world," he laughs.

At the time Isikah lived with the Mullys, he says, there were five hundred kids.

"What happened that first day?"

"Each kid did something to help me. They gave me clothes, books, pens, and showed me a bed in a dorm-like setting with lots of open space."

I'm still thinking he is one brave guy. I ask him what his daily routine was like.

"We woke up every morning at six to do chores. Chapel was open if we wanted to pray. We ate breakfast. Grades separated for classes. It was the biggest homeschool in the world. New kids worked together, and I didn't feel like I was alone. Every kid there helps each other. We all pitched in. We cleaned up after eating, washed dishes, and made sure everything was tidy."

"Sounds like a family."

"We were very disciplined. After school, we played soccer or volleyball, or swam in the river, or practiced karate or kung fu. I love kung fu."

He continues.

"A lot of people poured into me, teaching me, even helping

me learn to pray. Former street kids taught me about God. Daddy Mully changed all my perspectives of people. I had never seen good people like him. He helped me to trust in people again. He helped me to believe my life is worth something."

"And you believed it?"

"Daddy Mully always told us that our future is bright. We are going to be great people, in our families, leading the country of Kenya, and becoming part of a bigger change. I believed this big plan. God's big plans changed me. Imagine five hundred street kids and me—we felt loved and wanted, which we desperately needed.

"My Daddy Mully is a genius. He hires people from the community. He says the cycle of poverty is broken when we hire people, they make money, and kids remain safe in their homes and go to school in their own villages. He sees things, things that seem impossible. He communicates with God. I learned this from him. Even today I do things that seem impossible. I believe it can happen, and I work hard and am patient and believe."

Isikah worked so hard in school that he earned an international scholarship to attend Hope College in Holland, Michigan, where he earned a bachelor's degree in mechanical engineering.

I say, "I love that name, Hope College. It's perfect, especially for a guy who almost lost hope."

On that snowy night in that brightly lit Starbucks, I ask Isikah, "Can you imagine who you'd be if you hadn't taken the chance? It was scary, but you found yourself. You did it!"

"Many of my brothers and sisters, former street kids, study worldwide. We will make a difference; we believe it.

" THE HEALING PROCESS COMES FROM ACCEPTING WHO YOU ARE AND RECEIVING HOW YOUR FAMILY POURS INTO YOU. BUT YOU HAVE TO BE WILLING.

"I can tell you that adoption is to give you good hope and to help you become the person you are supposed to be. The healing process comes from accepting who you are and receiving how your family pours into you. But you have to be willing. That is the start of change."

ACCEPTANCE

A NATURAL REMEDY FOR PEACE

*In the book of life, the answers aren't
in the back.*

CHARLES M. SCHULZ

CHAPTER 26

SHE IS WHO SHE IS

Learn to befriend your experience.

BESSEL VAN DER KOLK

CAN I ACCEPT what happened to me? Will I be okay if I do? For some, acceptance may get rocky for a time; for others, it may be a nudge here and there. But accepting is discovering you don't have to rewrite your story . . . you just have to get right with it. That's when peace, purpose, and contentment show up and lead the way through. That's what happened to Cait.

Cait rarely thinks about being adopted. She's got other things on her mind—like travel. Over a late-afternoon lunch at Panera, she tells me she just completed a study abroad in Freiburg, Germany. Turns out traipsing around Germany has been on her bucket list since high school, and doing it unleashed the travel bug in her. Like the time she braved the IC, the high-speed train to Dortmund, by herself to see the soccer stadium and wander the city, seeing the ancient cathedrals and dropping into a *bäckerei* (bakery). Now she's hooked on travel. But there's more. Cait is energized by facts and research and things that interest her, such as why her face turns beet red if she drinks beer or any other alcohol. She discovered she has alcohol flush syndrome, compliments of her Chinese roots. She stays away. It's not a huge loss.

And then there's Quidditch.

Midbite into my baguette, I stop when I hear this curious word I've never heard before. I'm baffled and out of my league on this topic. Forgive me Harry Potter fans.

She says, "I am on the Support Staff for the Quidditch team at U of M." Her voice lights up as she tells me she commands the start of the game, keeps score, and other such duties.

I sit there, twisting my brain for a visual as she explains this game. Something about riding broomsticks, Chasers, Keepers, Seekers, and a Snitch, and a referee confined to the boundaries of the pitch. Sort of a fantasy-meets-athletic romp around a field between two competing teams. (Harry Potter fans, you get this, right?) Later I learned that this fictional game, invented by J. K. Rowling, is popular on many college campuses. Who knew?

The point is, a lot shapes who Cait is. At age twenty, she's a senior at University of Michigan, majoring in computer science, minoring in German, and living in a house with friends near campus. And while she claims she is an introvert and a facts-and-data girl, she can also be a fun time. Her friend, Lydia, confirms it later in a text, telling me Cait has an amazing sense of humor that comes out at the most surprising times—which makes it even more hilarious. Add musician, talented debater, and mischief-maker to the list.

Cait was adopted from China when she was eight months old. "I was called Xiqin Hong. The orphanage gave me my name. But I have a given name from my birth family that was lost."

She says thirteen families traveled together to China to adopt their children. The thirteen adopted kids played together at reunions and kept in close contact while they were in elementary and high school. So Cait has grown up with twelve kids from the same heritage, all with the same confusing information, estimated birth dates, and varying degrees of curiosity about their birth families. She tells me she interacted with them so much that she doesn't feel different. In fact, growing up this way normalized things for her.

"I know all the details from my parents. We don't talk about adoption a lot anymore."

This is common for some people who were adopted.

Some adoptees are extremely emotional about their separation story, some aren't, and others are somewhere in between. Cait explains she isn't emotional about it.

"I don't explore myself as much as others. I plow through," Cait explains. "It doesn't necessarily register that I need to think about these things. Like, my grandma died last year. I didn't take time to grieve. I'm not as cognizant of my emotions as some. I have a feeling it's my personality."

> BEING ADOPTED . . . IS WHAT WE MAKE OF IT, HOW WE CHOOSE TO RESPOND.

"For some people, it is their experience not to think about it, and that's okay," she says. "If there's not a lot of angst over your adoption, that's a blessing. Being adopted doesn't have to be hard. It's what we make of it, how we choose to respond."

She continues, "I wasn't overly interested in being adopted. I think, okay, I am here. I can't do anything about it. I just think I should probably move past that and not focus on it."

"And that's okay?" I ask.

"Yes. Being adopted generally doesn't define me. Sometimes

it does, like when I'm at the DMV and need extra documentation to get my driver's license," she adds.

"Ha. I get you." I have scrounged through files for passports and birth certificates and translations for the clerk at the DMV for my kids too.

Cait checks her phone. She has an online class shortly, so she has to go. She slides out of the booth and heads to her car, leaving me to think. I sit there, hovering over my notes, revisiting her energy and interests and thoughts. She knows her story; it makes sense to her, and she discovered that she doesn't have to rewrite her story in order to accept it. And accepting it doesn't limit her. She is who she is: broomsticks, German, and studying abroad; hardworking, smart, daughter, friend, student, American, Chinese heritage, and so much more.

Like Cait, you are in a dynamic season of life. A lot is going in and out of your mind and heart that shapes you: interests, faith, culture, heritage, family, friends, failures, successes, choices you make, hurts, confusion . . . and maybe Quidditch too.

CHAPTER 27

THE BEST OF HIM

There is a difference between solitude and isolation.
One is connected and one isn't. Solitude replenishes, isolation
diminishes.

HENRY CLOUD

IT WAS EARLY June when Zuri, a sprinter from a small Christian high school with a tiny team, ran her first state tournament in a suburb near Detroit. She remembers it being sunny at first, then a downpour, making everyone scrambled to take cover. When the officials put a hold on the track and field competition until the storm cleared, Zuri hung back with her coach and the other sprinters while her family fan base piled into their fifteen-passenger van to take refuge at a local Culver's just down the road. Pop-up storms are common in Michigan; Zuri prayed this one would blow over just as fast as it came. Qualifying at this level for her first time and competing in the 100- and 200-meter sprints was a dream come true, and she didn't want to lose out.

Zuri was fast! Gazelle fast. And as an adopted teen she began wondering where she got her speed and athleticism.

"I love to sprint," she tells me with a high-energy vibe. "It is my favorite thing in the world to do. Ever since I was little, I've been fast."

As she grew up, she became more and more athletic, as if it was meant to be, a gene-pool thing. She played center in volleyball and was one of the hardest hitters on the team. In basketball, she was always the first player down the court. But nothing beats running sprints in track, feet pounding, heart thumping out of her chest. She told me she felt like no one could catch her. Which came true when she broke four high school records.

When I meet with Zuri, she is seventeen and a high school senior—a gorgeous young black woman, vivacious, sensitive, and relatable. She smiles like something really great just happened to her, even if all you said was "Hi." Her friends say she's super athletic. And it's evident. She has legs a mile long and natural muscle power, but she works out to enhance her strength. She has six-pack abs without trying, but she is known to eat junk food and down a movie-size box of Hot Tamales cinnamon candy on occasion.

Zuri was born in the Deep South and raised in the North. Her birth mom, from Alabama, was raped at a party. When she found out she was pregnant, she was afraid and worried about what she was going to do. When she chose adoption, it was her way to protect her child. As a newborn, Zuri was adopted by a married couple from Michigan who were in their early thirties. Zuri jokes that she calls her mom and dad "my pasty parents," mainly because her mom jokes that if they had had biological kids, they'd have been freakishly white.

We laugh as we sit on the front porch of her house. Her youngest sister, three, denied access to her big sister, snuffs her nose against the window to watch us from inside. Zuri is the second oldest of six kids, all African American except her oldest sister. We sat outside on an April afternoon, a light rain sprinkling in the air. It took a while, but after several emails, we were finally meeting. Zuri wanted to talk about her birth father, how she never met him and knew very little about him. She was told her birth father was athletic. She knew that must be true based on her own athleticism. Then, two years ago, he became real to her when she was told he'd died. She was entering her junior year. Knowing she'd never meet him put her in an emotional funk.

"I had always wondered about my birth father," she says. "I was told I look like him and got my athletic genes from him too."

Her parents were open but didn't know much either.

"They told me what they knew."

She says her birth mom met a guy at a party and never saw him again. "When I was younger, I would ask my birth mom about him—we had an open adoption—and she would say she didn't want to talk about it."

As a young girl, Zuri assumed her mother's reluctance had something to do with her, so she stopped asking. But she didn't stop wondering.

"I wanted to meet him before it was too late."

She didn't know it already was.

"I remember the day like it was yesterday, when I was told my birth father had died. My parents called me into the kitchen."

They told Zuri the name of her birth father and explained that he lived in the same area as her birth mom. He had raped her birth mom, and many years later he had been killed in a random shooting.

"I was shaking," she says.

She tells me she ran to her room and threw herself on her bed, sobbing. In an instant, her life was turned upside down. She needed to think. She had to vent and breathe and smash her fists. Taking the lid off of something that big deserved it.

However, she didn't know how to grieve. She didn't know how to face the hard truth and ache that lingered. Instead, overwhelmed, she bottled the ache deep inside and isolated, one lonely day after the next. By herself, she couldn't make sense of things. But she didn't know enough to talk to someone, anyone. She always knew it was okay to wonder about her birth father or mother. But this was different. She had found out hard things that were not normal. That's when things got confusing.

Secretly, she wanted to know more. So during study hall one day, she decided to search for any remnants of him. It didn't take long to find his Facebook account.

"I found his Facebook page. He had worked at Arby's."

"Wow! That's something." I encourage her.

She nods. "It's weird, but our family had stopped at that same Arby's once while visiting my birth mom."

"You may have crossed paths?"

"Yes. So I messaged one of his Facebook friends at Arby's."

"Oh?"

"Surprisingly, she messaged me back! Learning something was better than nothing, I thought. She told me that my father was a good person. She made a point to say he had the best morals from anyone she'd ever met. A day wouldn't go by that he didn't say hello and see how she was doing. She told me, 'What happened to him messed up our whole town for a long time, and it wasn't right. But he wouldn't want us dwelling on that.' Hearing that from someone was comforting."

The only thing is, things didn't add up.

"What? Had he changed?" I ask.

"I don't know. Why would he do something awful to my birth mom years ago and today be considered a good man?"

It was more than confusing. Zuri wanted to believe her birth father had changed. She wanted to give him a second chance. But he was gone.

"The confusion burdened me so much that I became moody—and I am not a moody girl. I slipped into a funk, and I didn't know how to talk about my thoughts and feelings. So it all built up. I was feeling broken, like a piece was missing. For my junior and most of my senior year, I kept it all to myself."

She says she doesn't know how she did it. Every day felt like a dream and not real.

"I think I was trying to convince myself that everything would be fine if I blocked it out, that the next day would be back to normal. But one day turned into the next, and, well . . . I guess I was trying to cope with it."

"Months trying to block out reality? That's not good."

"Yeah. I felt awful. I felt sick and was always tired. I didn't want to do anything. And I complained about everything. My parents and girlfriends noticed too and asked me what was going on, but I hid the truth."

"Why hide the truth?" I ask.

"I don't know."

I move on. "So they thought you were just being moody?"

"Yes. But I slowly slipped into situational depression. My teachers even noticed that I wasn't my normal self. When I finally told my parents I was depressed, it was hard, but they were relieved. They just wanted to help me so much."

By now there was no way Zuri was going to get out of her funk on her own.

"I talked with a counselor for several months. She helped me sort out my feelings about my birth father."

> **WHEN YOU TELL SOMEONE YOU'RE AFRAID TO TALK, YOU'RE ACTUALLY LETTING THEM IN.**

She says coming to terms with the truth and accepting it was a good thing. Putting it all into words somehow worked her out of her depression. When you tell someone you're afraid to talk, you're actually letting them in. In Zuri's situation, she only wished she had gotten help earlier.

So I ask if she would have done anything differently. She looks down, searching the ground with her eyes, looking for an answer.

"I had to go through it. I had to grieve, even if I didn't know how. I needed to learn how to talk about it, to get comfortable with it, to accept it. It feels more natural now somehow. Now when it comes up, I'm . . ."—she hesitates to find the right word—"I'm more comfortable."

Zuri still has moments when she shuts herself in her room and wonders. But now she knows solitude and isolation are two different things. If you are isolating, you'll know. You will try to hide your hurt and confusion.

Zuri says, "Don't isolate. You may think it is better for you and your family if you keep things to yourself, but in the end it will only be worse. If you feel tired, sad, not interested in your friends or school activities, these are signs to get help fast. You don't have to get sick while your mind is trying to make sense and adjust to hard truths. People want to help you."

Because her family and friends stood with her during her

struggle, Zuri feels blessed. She got the help she needed and is on the other side of grief, feeling stronger than ever. She also feels blessed to have athletic genes. Zuri is an extraordinary runner and overall good athlete. That day in June at the stadium, the storm lifted. Zuri placed sixth, narrowly missing the top five in the state.

"I missed the top five by a tenth of a second," she says. "I'll be faster next time." She smiles.

"And your story? Where are you today?" I ask.

She thinks for a moment, then says, "It happened. I'm here. I'm the best of him."

Loss is a part of life, but it can be a double loss for anyone with adoption in their story. When a parent dies, it can feel as if you've been abandoned again. Losing a parent, aunt, or favorite pet may be extra tough. But just like Zuri, you don't need to isolate when you can't make sense of loss. You can learn to grieve what happened to you. You can sort things out with the help of others and accept fresh insight into your hurts.

CHAPTER 28

FINDING MYSELF

How beautifully you are learning the art of surrender,
the courage to let go, in the wild of your unknowns.

MORGAN HARPER NICHOLS

EIGHT YEARS AGO, when Josh lost his twin brother to suicide at sixteen, he never imagined how it would affect the rest of his life. He hesitated to talk about the details; the wound would always hurt. I didn't push. The pair had been adopted as babies in 1995 from the island country of Vietnam by parents from rural Minnesota, a small town of 1,500 where his adoptive parents were raised. Josh told me over several phone conversations from home that his life unfolded like most kids in rural Minnesota.

"We [Josh and his brother] had a pretty normal childhood. And just like any teenagers, we worried about things like prom, sports, friends, and hung out at Friday night football games, campfires, and church. It was a typical Midwest upbringing. It was what my parents grew up with, and they wanted that for us."

At twenty-four, Josh is smart, articulate and living in China to work on his master's degree. He says he enjoys hanging out with his Asian friends and going to dinner to get "hot pot," a Chinese meal where you dip raw food into boiling broth.

"It's like fondue," he says.

"It sounds delicious," I comment.

"It is. And with my American friends back home, I go ice fishing."

"Two totally different worlds," I smile.

He describes himself as a die-hard Minnesota Vikings fan. In China, he says, he wakes up at two in the morning to watch the Vikings play football live on his computer.

"I am just like everyone else. I love sports. I message my friends on Facebook about plays."

"And your brother?" I ask.

"He was really smart. He was my closest friend. We liked the same things but also had our own personalities. I know he was bullied a lot. We were two of the few Asians in a white community. Kids can be mean when they don't understand. They make fun of things. Some people go through that and are completely fine. It depends on the person. When everyone doesn't look like you, it can be hard."

Both Josh and his brother felt unacceptable in their teen years.

> **WHAT I HAVE REALIZED OVER TIME IS THAT THE ONLY PERSON ASKING IF I BELONG IS ME.**

"If you were to look at a selfie of me today with a group of my friends or family, you would think I belong. I look like a normal person spending time with loved ones. If you were to ask my friends or my mom or dad, they would say that there is nothing wrong with me and that I am even a fun person to be with. I mean, of course they would say I belong with them, but they are my family and friends. What I have realized over time is that the only person asking if I belong is me."

"Do you know why?" I ask, looking for insight.

"I have thought deeply about it and believe I was insecure with being myself, especially as a teen."

Josh traces his feelings back to a time he doesn't remember and struggles to put into words, a time that had a deep, significant impact on him, when his birth mother and father couldn't keep him.

"While I don't remember being a baby, I feel losing my first mother left me wanting and wondering and ultimately unable to accept myself for a long time because I falsely believed my birth parents didn't accept me. My twin brother also thought he was unacceptable and was insecure."

"You miss him a lot, don't you?" My voice quiets.

"Yes." His voice matches mine.

Josh has since learned that feelings of not belonging don't have to last and might not even be accurate.

"The truth is only one person sees me as unacceptable, and that's *me*."

Josh processed his brother's loss, his own adoption, and his Asian identity during a five-month study abroad in Singapore. It was an exciting time of his life because it was a chance to reinvent himself.

"I could be anyone I wanted. Nobody knew who I was or where I came from. My past became my own little secret, and for once in my lifetime it didn't define me."

He says the only thing his friends from Singapore knew was that he was an Asian who couldn't speak Chinese. (In other words, he wasn't a local.) He says living away from his friends and family back home wasn't easy, but he learned to get along with what came his way and made a lot of new friends along the way.

Being in a new setting really allowed him to essentially go on an adventure to find himself.

"When I returned from Singapore, I started thinking of myself in different ways. I had grown more confident in who I was. Suddenly, I was more than just an adopted person with a tragic past; I was a world traveler. I had immersed myself in Southeast Asia and had come back with crazy stories of being lost in an exotic culture, trying foreign foods, and connecting with wonderful people who lived in a different world from the one I had known my entire life."

Around this same time traveling in Asia, Josh also took a faith journey with God. He joined a Chinese Christian church near his university because he wanted to continue to develop other parts of himself, his Asian identity, and what it meant to be Christian.

"After my brother died, I wasn't sure where God fit into my life anymore. I had always had faith, but after what happened to Jason, my relationship with God seemed rather empty. I mean, why should I have faith in God if he can't protect the ones who love us the most?"

But after living in Singapore, Josh was surprised by how God used that time to heal him. Josh met friends who had incredible faith even when their lives weren't easy by Western standards. One friend confessed to him that she had lost her father at a young age. Being the oldest of three kids, she and her mom had scrambled every day to provide food and medical care for her siblings. She was attending college so she could make a better life and provide for her family. Yet through it all, her trust in God remained strong.

"One night I asked her how she could have faith after going through so much hardship in her life, and she replied, 'How can I afford not to have faith?' Her words left a deep impression on me. After that I thought differently about my own hardships."

He says her faith story gave him a deeper appreciation for the things that he has and for his friends and family.

"Today, more than ever, I have a lot of God in my life. As for my Asian identity, I really wanted to continue where I left off in Singapore. So I started learning Mandarin while I was there and wanted to continue it in the States."

He says Mandarin is a hard language, and he has a lot to learn, but he's reached the point where he is comfortable getting around speaking just Chinese. "It has been a really rewarding experience learning a new language, and it has allowed me to connect with different people and cultures that I never would have thought possible."

Now that he's older, he says he sees a lot of adoptees going through similar things he went through, struggling to figure out what *belonging* means. He says he's very empathetic toward people. Recently he stepped into a new role as a volunteer mentor to adopted teens and young adults.

"I speak at Vietnamese Culture Camp and talk about the problems I've faced. I am also a moderator for an adoptee Facebook group and meet adoptees from all over the world this way. If there are ways I can give back, I want to give back. When you've lived through depression, racial inequity, and mental health issues in your family, you see the world from a different lens. My brother committed suicide. It is a very personal story and very difficult to talk about. But I can talk about myself and the journey I took to realize I do belong."

It hasn't been an easy journey for Josh, and it's a journey that he says isn't finished.

"Adoptees are like anyone else. We try to do the best with what we have. I hope that by sharing where I am now I can help those who are also walking a similar path and help them through. We are all people filled with feelings, emotions, thoughts, and insecurities."

If Josh says life is worth living after so much loss, then I'm listening, and I hope you are too.[1]

CHAPTER 29

THE DRAFT

Working hard is important.
But there is something that matters more:
Believing in yourself.

J. K. ROWLING

HAVE YOU EVER thought life is just random? Like, sit back and things will just happen for you? Well, it doesn't work that way. At least, that's what I learned from Zach, who discovered in sixth grade that it takes hard work to believe in yourself and achieve your dreams.

Does Zach have a secret formula for success? Sort of. He started setting goals for himself, using what he calls the "Post-it Note Pyramid" plus "I will" statements—his own version of a responsibility chart. He writes goals on Post-its, sticks them on his bedroom wall in the shape of a pyramid, and—every morning, noon, and night—he sees them there in plain sight, reminding him that life is not random. He works on the bottom-layer goals first because meeting those goals will get him to the next level. His ultimate goal is the last sticky on top, the icing on the cake. That one could take years. And it has. Five years ago, when Zach was a chunky middle schooler living on chicken nuggets and Instagram, he didn't care about much. Today he's on track to pitch D-1 baseball. That's big! The top sticky note? To be drafted into the major league. That's even bigger!

Zach was "drafted" by die-hard New York Yankees fans Alicia and Brian when he was a ten-month-old baby in Komsomolsk-on-Amur in the Khabarovsk Region of the Russian Far East—one of the most remote parts of the world. To put the remoteness into perspective, imagine being on the Trans-Siberian Railway in a sleeping car for six nights, crossing ten time zones stretching from Moscow through Russia's extensive Siberian frontier, and ending your trip at the border of China. The distance is staggering, double that of a trip across the United States. The odds of being adopted from such a place are as slim as becoming a major-league baseball player. Zach plans to beat the odds twice.

Today, at sixteen, Zach is a junior in high school and much like any other kid. He's a pitcher, a dang good one. He says he plays club and high school ball, regularly throwing ninety-mile-per-hour pitches. I did a little research and found out that's better than Justin Verlander pitched in high school. You know, MLB player Justin Verlander? Houston Astros? World Series 2017 champs? That's fast.

It's eight o'clock on a Thursday evening in May when Zach calls me on FaceTime from New Jersey, forty-five minutes outside New York City. Boonton, his hometown, he tells me, is a two-by-two-mile suburban square featuring Walmart, Dunkin Donuts, four gas stations, and a town hall that closely resembles the town hall in *Back to the Future*, clock tower and all. I ask Zach what his town is known for, and he jokes, "Absolutely nothing."

On the screen, Zach looks like any teen guy. He's growing into his six-foot frame but still has a boyish face. We both adjust camera positions so we can get the best view of each other. He's holding his tan-and-white beagle, Dash, on his lap and quickly introduces me to the burly six-year-old pup—who pokes his nose into the camera lens, says hello, then quickly jumps down and dashes off in pursuit of Dad's voice in the background. Zach's mom is online too. The two sit next to each other at a cleared dining table in their kitchen. The three of us hit it off immediately, as if we're just hanging out after dinner.

Zach is one of the youngest participants in this book. Actually, he was fifteen when we first connected. Since then he's had a birthday and a buzz mullet. I can hardly tell the difference until he pulls his curly brown hair over to the side to reveal his smooth, clean-shaved scalp. He's left the hair on the back and top to grow into a soft spill of curls. The "bold 'do move," I'll call it, is a concoction made up by Zach and his friends. He says with a grin that it's a sort of solidarity thing, something to stave off boredom. As he messes with his hair, I notice a collection of bracelets on his wrist. Among the bunch are NY Yankees, no surprise, and a red, black, white and yellow one representing the University of Maryland, a recent purchase to celebrate his verbal commitment to pitch for the University of Maryland when he graduates—the second from the top goal on the Post-it Note Pyramid.

"The hair thing makes me think you have some crazy friends," I say. "How would they describe you?"

"They'd say I provide comic relief but that I am also insightful and serious. I'm the one in the group that usually tells them when they are making a stupid decision. Someone's got to be the dad of the group." He laughs.

But it's no joke. He seems mature for his sixteen years.

"I think I get along with so many kids because I've played on so many sports teams. I guess I adapt pretty easily."

He reflects on years of being dropped off to a new team and a bunch of new kids from all over the place, whom he has never met. That's the thing about baseball—the lasting friendships, *Sandlot*-type friendships: crazy, goofy kids learning to count on each other both on and off the field. Most of his friends have come from his hometown teams, travel teams, and school teams. In the best possible way, teams have helped shape Zach's social confidence.

"When did you start playing baseball?" I ask.

"I asked my parents if I could play T-ball when I was four. And then little league. And then I played parks-and-rec baseball from five to twelve. I was also on our town's all-star teams from ten to twelve, when I could start trying out for them. Then I played for the town travel team from eight to twelve in the spring and fall. Once I was thirteen, I started playing for my club team, Wladyka Baseball. I also play for the Tri-State Arsenal Scout team, which is a national team that plays in tournaments all over the country."

"Woah," I say. "That's a huge commitment."

He continues, "After eighth grade, I realized that I needed to start focusing on my pitching mechanics after my pitching coach told me that my fastball velocity was very high for my age. My parents and I knew that it was time to make an investment in my future as a pitcher."

I had no idea baseball was anything more than a bat and ball and Big League Chew. I'm out of my league when Zach and his mom both explain that baseball requires brainpower and that it's very strategic. Players have to be laser-focused and quick-thinking. It's very difficult, but over time, each player gains the knowledge needed to be successful. Beyond that, it is time-consuming.

"I've had to learn to lift," Zach says. "You have to be strong to be a pitcher. During the year, I play spring, summer, and fall baseball. January to March is all about strength and conditioning three times a week, along with pitching training two times a week. In the spring, I have my high school baseball season from March to June and train at home when I can, two to three times a week. Summer ball runs from June to July, and I also work out two to three times a week. We get the month of August off. From September to October is fall ball season, and I work out two to three days a week. My arm gets shut down in November and December, and I focus just on strength and agility training three to four times per week."

"Okay. Wow!" I exclaim. "You eat, breathe, and sleep this stuff. Sorry, I never knew so much hard work went into the sport. It's obviously paying off. Your fastball is fast!"

"The fastest I've been clocked at was ninety miles per hour as a sophomore in high school," Zach says. "Prior to that, I topped at eighty-eight miles per hour in a tournament."

"Tell me about the day you pitched ninety miles per hour."

"It was cool."

"Let me get this straight. You're pitching 'Justin Verlander–like' when he was sixteen, a guy that led the Houston Astros to win the World Series in 2017, and it's just cool. Seriously?"

"He's pitching one hundred miles per hour now, but yeah. I've got some work to do. I found out that my coach saw me pitching ninety miles per hour for months before I knew. Ninety is a baseline for college coaches and recruiters," he says casually.

"Ninety says you're getting there. It didn't mean as much as I thought, but it meant I had to keep improving."

Coaches and college recruiters are noticing, he says. He's come a long way from being the last kid to be picked for teams.

"I used to goof around a lot. I was a screwball. I wasn't serious about anything. I was short and chubby and didn't care."

It changed when he was at a Yankees game and said to himself, "I want to do that!" That's when his passion for baseball grew into so much more. He got serious. He started to hit the weights, adjusted his diet, and felt a lot better physically, mentally, and emotionally.

"I have a warrior mindset now. I have an incredibly competitive nature."

His mom quickly interrupts to add, "He's humble, though."

"I pitch with the mindset that if you lose your focus, or if you miss one thing on delivery, you will throw a wild pitch."

I nod. "You seem very focused for your age."

"I am," Zach agrees. "I am very self-motivated too. I started writing goals for myself—'I will eat healthy. I will out-work, out-play, and out-pitch everyone. I will play varsity baseball. I will play D-1 college baseball. I will play professional baseball.' They've been posted there since sixth grade."

Zach continues. "I look at my Post-it pyramid and keep striving for the next goal. Bring it on," he says. "I don't look behind me. I focus on the present so I can look forward to the future. I learn from my mistakes and never make the same mistake twice."

He pulls Dash, the dog, back onto his lap and rubs his floppy ears.

"Are you teachable?" I ask.

"Yes, 100 percent," he says. "There should always be room for growth and development. When I make mistakes—moral, ethical, or emotional—it is my job to listen to my coaches and implement what I've learned. If you are not going to change after an apology, then you are not going to grow. When you make mistakes, learn from them. Pitching coaches are always fixing small areas of my mechanics. You have to adjust in an instant. It's the same way in life."

"What happens when you make it to the next level of the Post-it Note Pyramid?" I ask.

"Anything in life is a constant grind; you have to always be chipping away," Zach replies. "There is always something more. Never be satisfied. Stay hungry."

I nod. "Do you think you got this growth mindset from your parents?"

"Yes."

I smile. "I can see from your mom's expression that she really believes in you and is proud of you."

I notice him pause and chew on his lower lip while thinking.

"None of this would be possible without them," Zach says. "Just being around them has helped me grow and develop as a human. They have sacrificed so much for me and my training besides just money. They've given up socializing with their friends, made countless drives to different facilities, booked flights and hotel stays for various tournaments, paid travel ball fees and equipment costs. Every year I help pay for some of the new, expensive equipment I need, including gloves, bats, batting gloves, turf shoes, cleats, et cetera. I help them as much as I can."

"I can tell you are close with your parents."

Zach glances at his mom. "My parents can be hard on me at times, but they want the best for me. It can be pretty hard, but I know it's worth it."

"And your birth parents in Russia—do you think about them?"

"It's like, *Oh, am I adopted?* I am not personally interested in meeting my birth family. That may sound bad, but that's how I feel now. I have never really wondered." He pauses to think. "Am I weird or something?"

> **FEELINGS COME AND GO. AND IF THEY SURFACE, IT'S SO YOU CAN SORT THEM OUT.**

I laugh and shake my head. "No, you're not weird. You're normal. There is a range of responses that adoptees experience, and it depends on the person. You may be at one end of the continuum today, not thinking about them, and that may change in the future if your curiosity stirs. Who knows? Feelings come and go. And if they surface, it's so you can sort them out. You're pretty busy and fulfilled right now. Your mind is preoccupied with good things."

I can tell he is trying to sort it out on the spot. Trying to make a connection to the past.

"I am fiercely independent," he admits. "Maybe I got that from being in the orphanage?" he questions with a wondering look in his eyes.

"He's Russian stoic," his mom adds.

Zach quickly agrees. "Yeah, I am Russian stoic."

Later, I looked it up. *Stoic* means uncomplaining, patient, calm, and unexcitable. Hmm. Great traits for a pitcher, I thought.

"Are you proud of your Russian heritage?" I ask.

"Yes," Zach says. "It sets me apart. I find it very interesting. It is what makes me *me*. It is a part of my uniqueness."

In fact, Zach's screen saver on his phone is of him, all geared up, winding up a pitch, with the Russian flag dropped into the background. A little something his friends put together for him when he chose Maryland.

Zach's advice: "Don't count yourself out, ever! Find your passion. Set goals. Go for it!"

Most fifteen-year-olds pitch, on average, seventy miles per hour. D-1 pitchers throw eighty-seven to ninety-five miles per hour on a consistent basis. It's highly likely that, as Zach's body and skill mature, his pitching velocity and accuracy will too. As for the Post-it at the top of the pyramid? He'd like to go pro. Stay tuned; 0.5 percent of high school pitchers will be drafted, and only 10 percent of that figure will be signed. But the kid born in remote Russia and raised in New Jersey is going for it. He's set his sights high, and he's dreaming big. It just goes to show, the important thing in life isn't where you're from. The important thing in life is who you are and what you do with the life you were entrusted with.

CHAPTER 30

PERMISSION TO GRIEVE

It takes strength to face our sadness and to grieve and to let our grief and our anger flow in tears when they need to.
It takes strength to talk about our feelings and to reach out for help and comfort when we need it.

MISTER ROGERS

WHEN KIRA WAS seventeen, she had AP English to tackle, homecoming plans to make, and basketball practice on her mind. She was smart, athletic, and by binge-watching YouTube tutorials, she taught herself how to play the ukulele. Distracted by life and TikTok, she never imagined she would grieve anything at her age. Then one night—she can't explain why—she began weeping for her birth father, a man she had never met. Feelings surfaced that she didn't know she had.

Kira always knew about her birth story, but as a young girl she rarely thought about it. At fifteen, her parents hired a search agency to find her birth mother, and within a month she had good and bad news. The searcher had been successful. Her birth mother was alive and had two additional little girls. At the same time, Kira also learned her birth father was dead. As much as she wanted to know about her separation story, she just wasn't ready to face the loss. So she buried the information in a large yellow envelope at the bottom of her mom's sock drawer and forgot about it. She says there was nothing she could do anyway. When we sat down at her house to talk about that night, the tears came, and so did what this man means to her.

"So, why now?" I ask. "Why grieve a man you never knew?"

"Because I'm half him," she says.

"That's huge!"

She begins to fill in the details and how her emotions erupted unexpectedly.

It was a Friday night. She had been sitting on her twin bed, lamplight shining over her shoulder while the rest of the room was dark, moody. Her mom and dad had gone out for the night with friends.

"I was alone in my own space listening to the YouTube video 'Who Am I?' from the musical Annie. Not the classic—the new one," she clarified. "Oh, well, I love them both."

The lyrics made her nostalgic. "I do that sometimes. I grab my baby book, the one with everything in it—well, most everything, if you know what I mean—and I listen to music and wonder. I treasure my baby book," she says. "It is a Creative Memories album of me—when I learned how to swim and when I taught myself how to ride a two-wheeler. I was three, by the way," she proudly says, as if the milestone had happened yesterday.

Normally, those pages brought back sweet memories for Kira. She says her childhood was a blast. But this time was different.

"This time, after I had flipped through the album, I looked down and studied my veins on my wrist and the blood flowing through them from people I never met." She wondered which traits she had gotten from her birth father and which ones from her birth mother.

"I'll never sort it out, I know."

Kira was born in Russia in December 2001. At four months old she was brought to a baby home in Ishim, a small city just over the Ural Mountains in Siberia where the European and Asian continents divide. She likes to tell her girlfriends she's Asian even though she is 100 percent of Eastern European descent. In the baby home, she was placed with newborns and infants in a warm nursery with ten cribs lined side by side, like one of Kira's favorite childhood books, *Madeleine*. In 2003 she was adopted.

"What happened after digging into your baby album?" I ask.

"I jumped off my bed and ran to my parents' room. I opened up my mom's dresser drawer and dug out the yellow envelope that held the search documents."

Once she returned to her room and flicked on the lights, she plunked down on the floor and carefully laid out each page.

"I hadn't read through them in two years," she said. "The information hit me differently than when I was fifteen, when it had first arrived. Two years ago, I didn't think much about it. Now that I am older, I think deeper about things. I didn't want to think about my birth family back then," she admits. "It was cool to know, but I didn't really care."

Then something changed. Kira knew the details of her adoption, but something new was happening now: she was feeling them.

"That night, while rereading the papers, I felt guilty. Somebody in my life was dead, and I hadn't given it a second thought. I always knew I would never meet him," she says. "We lived an ocean apart. But now I *knew* I would never meet him, ever!"

Tears slipped down her cheeks for a father she'd never know.

As she swiped away the warm dampness with her hand she murmured, "Sometimes being adopted just doesn't feel right."

Surrounded by her baby book and the search pages, she said it was as if her two worlds were colliding.

"It all made sense. I was living this beautiful life with a hole in my heart. I couldn't put it into words; I just sat there crying, missing my father, missing the one who made me possible, and missing a part of myself. No one was there to talk me out of my emotions. It was my grief and no one else's. And I didn't want to share it with anyone else, not yet. It feels selfish to say this, but sometimes you need to wrestle with things by yourself and in the moment."

When her tears subsided, a surprising idea came to her. To honor her birth father she would write something or create something as a reminder that she is thinking of him, that he is somebody, and that she hasn't forgotten.

"I grabbed my sketch pad off my desk, flipped to a clean page, and reached for my favorite black pen."

She says her hand began to move and create, and the page filled quickly.

"I'd never drawn anything like it. It was an epitaph—a memorial to my birth father."

She wrote his name, Sergei, in script, and then the dates he was born and died.

"Next I wrote, 'May you rest in peace. You will always have a special place in my heart, your daughter, Kira.'"

Carefully, she tore the page from the pad, cleared away the mess on her dresser to make a place, and laid it there. Months later, she says, it still sits next to her Sony alarm clock. I took a look.

"Now I can have a time of remembrance whenever I want to."

That night, alone in her bedroom, Kira realized she might not ever get answers in this life. When she gets to heaven though, she plans to ask God about her birth father and what he looks like and what he is like.

"I can't find that out on earth. He's gone. So the drawing makes sense to me. It is a tangible way I can show he has a special place in my heart and that I am half him."

> **TO GRIEVE, NO MATTER HOW, IS A CHANCE TO FIND PEACE.**

Kira had thought nothing about her birth father until one day, suddenly, she was flooded with questions and thoughts of him. "Do I look like him? Am I like him? I didn't let my grief consume me. It comes at random times for a while and then leaves. Maybe we are meant to grieve and say goodbye so we can heal."

I think Kira stumbled into something good: that to grieve, no matter how, is a chance to find peace.

What do you know about grieving the loss of your birth mother or father, even if they are still living? Perhaps creating a tangible memorial might bring closure. If that idea appeals to you, you could try:

- Lighting a memorial candle. Many churches offer candles that you can light in memory of a lost one.
- Planting a tree in remembrance of your roots.
- Asking your church family to hold a small, private, special service.
- Writing lyrics to a song.

Regardless of what you choose to do, grieving is the path to peace and healing. Grieving allows us to unlock the tears and confusing emotions that are waiting to be released.

CHAPTER 31

I LOVE MY FAMILY AND KNOW I BELONG

Remember the past, love the present, look toward the future, never forget, always forgive, don't regret decisions, live every day as if it's your last.

NISHAN PANWAR

HANNAH WAS BORN in Nanning, China. Her sister, Samantha, was born in Nanchang, China, three years later. Their parents adopted the two girls on two separate trips, when each was around eleven months old, and a family was born. Now nineteen, Hannah sits across from me at the restaurant. Her mom sits next to her. They agreed to meet me for dinner after Hannah's flute lesson. I hadn't seen Hannah or her family in years. The first time we met, she was only eight. We had concocted a dog party for their collie, Princess, and our collie, Riley, both puppies and cousins from the same kennel. So in a way, we are related.

Hannah glows. It's just who she is. She has a presence about her, and her face lights up when you meet her. Her smile welcomes you into her world. Photography, hanging out with friends, traveling with her family, and acting keep her happy and busy. But it didn't happen overnight or without work.

I glance across the table at a confident young lady, but Hannah assures me she wasn't always this way.

"I was very quiet as a teen. I hated public speaking and always got anxious talking in big crowds. I started acting in eighth grade, so I would have been around fourteen. My acting instructor pushed me to be confident and comfortable in my own skin. He also taught me to project my voice, which I could also use in life and school."

She tells me it was hard for her to be assertive and confident in herself before she started acting lessons.

And as for being adopted, she says it is hard at times.

"My past is how I got to be where I am today. There are going to be challenges and unanswered questions in my life, and as much as I want the answers, I don't want to let that blind me from what I am able to create now."

Hannah has the usual questions about her birth family and an occasional nudge to wonder about why her birth parents would give up their baby. But all in all, she's just an American Asian girl in love with her family.

I get the feeling she wishes other people would see it her way. She's bumped up against some interesting and sometimes annoying scenarios, like the time she and her sister, at ages eighteen and fifteen, arrived in Hawaii for vacation with their grandma and aunt.

She fills me in. "I heard, 'Samantha K., please return to the luggage carousel,' over the loudspeaker."

"That's your sister. What was going on?" I ask.

"Samantha had left her carry-on back at the luggage carousel. We were standing in Honolulu International Airport, surrounded by travelers. We had just arrived in Oahu, Hawaii, with our grandma and aunt for a week. Our aunt told us to stay put. She and grandma took off to get the carry-on."

"Sounds pretty simple."

"After they disappeared into the crowd, we stood by our luggage on our cell phones and waited. When they didn't return, I got worried, so we walked over to an airport security guard to ask for help. That's when I spotted them on the other side near the luggage carousel. But the security guard stopped us."

"That seems odd to me."

"He told us to wait and asked us, 'Is that your family?' He looked at us and looked at them on the other side. I looked at him and wondered, why are you asking me this? Of course that is my family. Then he said, 'Are you sure you want to go with them?' I said, 'Yes! That's our grandma and aunt!'"

She says it was a relief when the security guard let them go. It wasn't until they were in the rental car that she realized what this guy was thinking. He thought something was wrong.

"I thought, *Could it be because my sister and I are Chinese, and our grandma and aunt are not Chinese?* I was slowly catching on."

It didn't make sense to the security guard, and it didn't make sense to her that it didn't make sense to him.

"I had never thought of my family as different."

Then there was the time at the nail studio when she and her mom got their nails done.

"The first time my mom and I got a manicure, the ladies insisted I was Vietnamese. 'She Vietnamese,' they said, shaking their heads and smiling. 'She have Vietnamese eye and skin color.' My mom tried to explain, 'But she was born in China. I know.' Then my mom recalled that I was born close to the

Vietnamese border. 'She Vietnamese!' they insisted. I thought, Now I am Vietnamese with a white mom!"

Then there is the classic question from strangers that comes up way too often: "Are you two sisters?"

"I just want to say for the last time, yes, we are sisters! We will always be sisters!" I hear her. That one is pretty common. We all share in that sense of *ugh*.

She takes a breath and reassures me that life isn't about all these odd exchanges with strangers. In fact, adoption doesn't define her.

"Really, I don't think about these things like other people do. I focus on the family I have right now. I love my family and have never thought of them differently. Besides, it is hard to focus on what might have been. It's hard to fill in the blanks when everything is blank."

> **I DON'T LOOK LIKE MY PARENTS OR MY AUNT OR GRANDMA, BUT TO ME, LOOKS AREN'T EVERYTHING. WHAT IS EVERYTHING TO ME IS JUST BEING WITH THEM.**

At barely five foot two, almost as tall as her mom, Hannah and her mother bump shoulders and smile. "Yes, I have Asian features. My mom and dad don't. But they have everything I need and want, and that is enough for me. They have helped shape who I am and encouraged my gifts. Yes! I don't look like my parents or my aunt or grandma, but to me, looks aren't everything. What is everything to me is just being with them."

A few months after our visit, I email Hannah, curious to find out what she's up to now, recalling what she said about not letting the past blind her from what she is able to create today. She tells me she's a Disney princess. No, really. I launched in with a bunch of questions.

"Who's your favorite?"

"Mulan, because she is brave and fights for what she believes in. I also find myself in her, and she is one of the very few princesses who look like me." I notice the resemblance.

"Events? Shows?"

Hannah tells me all this and more.

"Just the other weekend I did an event and was able to interact with families who are impacted by cancer or terminal illness. One of the families had a child who was suffering from brain cancer and only had a few weeks left to live. The princesses were able to put a smile on her face and be her forever sisters.

"I never would have thought I would have the opportunity to be an actual princess. I love every aspect of bringing magic to families who might need it."

Hannah's also a student ambassador at her college.

She's flipped her teen script. She wants to live confidently. She wants to create a life that is worthy. And to do that she is using her voice.

CHAPTER 32

YOU GET ME

A day without a friend is like a pot without
a single drop of honey left inside.

A. A. MILNE

TRIPLETS! I LOOK around the well-worn oak kitchen table at three fourteen-year-old faces and speculate. Hmmm. What are the chances? Could they be fraternal triplets? I look closer at two girls and one boy who look nothing alike.

"I am fourteen, my sister is fourteen, and my brother is fourteen." Kennedy, sitting in the chair closest to me, offers up an explanation. "We are all in ninth grade. We are all 100 percent Chinese. But we are not all from the same birth family or province of China."

"Ah." I smile, beginning to grasp the gist of this combo of teens, who, along with their mom, Lesley, have invited me into their warm, eat-in kitchen on a wintery afternoon. The table is covered with textbooks and computers, and the three teens have just finished another day of school.

Just like triplets, these three have a special bond between them. They claim the same friends, hang out together, and homeschool together. They connect, most of the time. They have each other. Yet each makes sure I know they are very much their own person. Ezra, wiry and thin with a contagious smile, admits he's the prankster of the bunch. He appears laid back. Kennedy, who exudes confidence and, I'm told, is strong-willed, excels in school and loves dogs. Harper, a gentle soul at first sight, enjoys dance—but is known to be stubborn.

I wonder, how did these three arrive in a small Midwestern town at different points on the calendar and different years and turn out to be the same ages?

"I came home first," Kennedy explains, "just before my first birthday."

I sense she's the leader of the pack, the spokesperson for the group. The nods confirm I am right on. Later I find out she's actually the youngest, but they are all within months of each other.

"I was four when I traveled with my parents to China to pick up Ezra. He was four too," Kennedy says as she locks eyes with her brother, then with her sister. "I was seven when we traveled for Harper, who was also seven."

I turn, raising my eyebrows to Mom, who sits on my left. "Was this planned?"

"No!" she laughs. No, no, no with an exclamation mark, while shaking her head, still trying to figure out how it did happen. "None of it was planned."

Yet here they are, three kids transplanted at different times into the same family, kids who happen to be the same age and miraculously click.

Kennedy thinks back.

"It had to be super scary to be so young and uprooted from all you had ever known," Kennedy says of Ezra and Harper. "Harper was seven when she became my sister. I think she was comforted by having a girl the same age for a sister when she joined our family. How confusing it must have been for both my brother and my sister to go with strangers. They were both very brave. Sometimes my sister and I talk about how different our lives would be if we hadn't been adopted. We wouldn't know each other, and we are super close."

The girls have a healthy connection, consider each other safe, and can open up with each other about anything. As for their brother, if they are safe, he is safe.

"So what's the secret to being super close?" I ask.

"I don't know," Harper ponders.

Kennedy says, "We rarely fight. Some of our friends fight all the time."

Ezra jokes, "I've got no clue."

"So it's real. You all get along?" I push.

"Yep," they say after a little poking about disagreeing about playlists.

Stories bounce around the table like a hot potato at a campfire. One takes violin lessons, one takes guitar, and one dances. All of them are in church theater and Odyssey of the Mind. Harper is in driver's training. The three are only months apart in age and in the same grade, but they make sure I know they like different things.

"I like dogs," Kennedy says.

In the bedroom nearby, a two-year-old Australian labradoodle, Fig, is trying to jump his fence. He can't stand being cooped up and away from the kids. Kennedy takes the gate down, and Fig skitters into the kitchen, nails scratching on the hardwood floor for balance. I've just lost everyone's attention to this beloved ball of blond fluff.

"I begged for a dog, " Kennedy says while gently commanding Fig to sit, spin, and lie down.

She continues, "Ezra is a Lego master and has a black belt in tae kwon do. He may study engineering someday." She looks over at Ezra, and he nods. "And for some reason, he calls Fig 'Pickles.'"

"Pickles?" I smile, raise my brows, and smirk. "Verrrry odd."

"Yeah, Pickles," he says. "It's funny." The girls laugh. His role as family jokester is solid.

With a quick glance over at Harper, Kennedy adds, "My sister loves dance and kids. She has a compassionate heart and may teach or become a pediatric nurse someday."

These kids get each other. What they go through, they go through together. They aren't just sparring partners; they infuse encouragement, acceptance, and friendship into their relationship.

It's almost 5:00 p.m. Harper quietly heads upstairs to her room. An older brother, a big burly dude, blows in from the garage into the kitchen and places a grocery bag of avocados and Tostitos on the island. A split second later, Ezra skirts around the chair and slips from the table to the kitchen island to help prepare guacamole. Within seconds, knives chop onions and bowls are pulled from cabinets like a well-choreographed skit. It's Mexican night.

Gradually, we all make our way around the kitchen island. A blur of hands squeeze ripe, yellow lemon halves over freshly mashed avocados. A good dash of salt and pepper follows. Kennedy reaches for the ground beef in the fridge. Soon the pan sizzles and the meat browns for tacos. A pile of plates fills the counter. It's elbow-to-elbow fun. The crew clicks like a take-out team at Taco Bell.

That's when I realize, this isn't forced family fun. I can see these kids have something special. They have each other, they share a common heritage, and they share a similar loss.

I copy down the guac recipe: loads of mashed avocados, squeezed lemons, salt and pepper to taste. And I think to myself, there's really no exact recipe, just a mix of good things like this sibling recipe of love and support.

"We are all thankful we have each other and are super close," Kennedy says while browning the beef. "Sometimes we talk about what we would have missed out on if we had not been adopted from China. Compared to a life in an orphanage in China . . . we would have missed out on almost everything most people take for granted. I wouldn't have any of my siblings, especially my sister and brother from China. I wouldn't have my amazing family. I wouldn't have my dog. I wouldn't have been able to experience camping, playing violin, gymnastics, dance, or my church and my friends."

FRIENDS AND FAMILY HAVE YOUR BACK ON PURPOSE AND BY DESIGN. HUMANS AREN'T MEANT TO BE ALONE.

Friends—that's what Ezra, Kennedy, and Harper are to each other. Not just siblings but also close friends. And let me level with you: Friends are so important. They give you emotional support when needed. They help you grow your confidence, give you advice and encouragement, help you destress, and help you to be your best both mentally and physically. They also help you sort out choices that could be wrong and ugly. Friends and family have your back on purpose and by design. Humans aren't meant to be alone.

We were all designed by God to crave the benefits of friendship. Whether you have a built-in friend group at home like Ezra, Kennedy, and Harper, or have one good friend like Paul in an earlier story, it can make all the difference. How to find friends? Pick up a hobby. Join a youth group at church. Start biking, hiking, or climbing. What about cupcake wars? Photography lessons? In other words, do what you like with people who are like-minded. Then be a friend. Hone it. You'll get back as much as you give.

CHAPTER 33

THANKFUL

As long as thanks is possible, then joy is always possible.

ANN VOSKAMP

MORGAN WAS BORN in Golyshmanovo, a village in the Tyumen region of Siberia, east of the Ural Mountains, where elk and lynx and brown bears roam the forest, and farmland spans for miles in the flatlands.

As a small girl, she lived in her grandmother's apartment with her mom and her two younger sisters . . . until suddenly they didn't. Their apartment was sold for rubles to pay off debts, and mom and the girls were sent away to find a place to live. They were homeless—so the documents say. Morgan was seven. Her sister Katya was four. Her baby sister, Valeria, was a newborn just four months old. Morgan was too young to comprehend how much peril her family was in. Then one day their mom dropped the girls at a shelter in the village while she looked for a place to live. One day turned into several. Then a week went by. She didn't return, not even for a last goodbye. It's hard to understand. The girls were separated. Morgan and Katya were placed together in the village orphanage. Their infant sister was placed in a baby home four hours away. They were likely never to be reunited again.

Jump-cut to today. At twenty-five, Morgan lives with Katya and their adoptive mom in their spacious three-bedroom townhouse near Westport, Connecticut, close to the beaches of New York Sound and the excitement of New York City, a one-hour train ride away. With everything at her fingertips, Morgan has since become a fashionable city girl, drawn to design and beauty. Her days are filled with clients and shadowing designers at the upscale furniture store where she works. She's doing what she loves. But she tells me she's just as happy relaxing on the beach in an American Eagle T-shirt, shorts, and Michael Kors flip-flops purchased from an outlet mall nearby, with her girlfriends of course. She has an amazing friend group, she says. Her mom is her constant. Oh, and eating pasta, no sauce. She says she gets her love for pasta from her Italian cousins.

When I asked Morgan what one word sits on her heart today, she says, "I am thankful." She started sensing the fullness of hope and beauty in her life in high school, about seven years after she was adopted.

"I started feeling thankful in high school," she says. "I realized that my life is likely better than what I would have had. Everything has somehow worked out as it should. I am thankful for my life and my family. If I were back in Russia, I don't know where I would be. I am happy it turned out the way it did."

When I first met Morgan, she was eleven going on twelve. She was in sixth grade, with a gentle spirit and an American Girl Doll look-alike, jammies and all.

My husband and I had knocked on the door to her family townhouse that day, with her baby sister, Valeria, now five, standing by my side holding my hand—the sister she never forgot about, but never expected to see again.

"I remember my mom got a call," Morgan says. "I learned my sister was in the States. I was so excited to reunite with my baby sister because I had only seen her when she was first born."

> **THE MORE THANKFUL SHE IS, THE MORE TRAUMA'S CLAMMY HANDS LOOSEN THEIR HOLD ON HER.**

Reuniting the girls was miraculous. It was one of those many bright spots Morgan has collected that makes her thankful. That's the thing: Morgan is able to be thankful even though she has a history of extreme loss and trauma. She remembers what happened to her as a little girl. She doesn't deny whom she lost, either. She will never forget. But the more thankful she is, the more trauma's clammy hands loosen their hold on her.

"I don't remember much," she always tells me when we see each other. This time she remembered a little more than the last. "I was too young to make sense of it. I was seven. We were still with our mom at that point. I remember a little about our house, that we were there together sometimes."

We talk about arriving at the orphanage.

"I was scared," she recalls. "I remember the orphanage. A woman said my mom would come back and we would go home with her. I hoped, but then it didn't happen. It all happened so fast. Katya and I were separated in the orphanage by age."

"You mean you were living in different parts of the orphanage?" I clarify.

"Yes. We had visiting hours. Katya would come to my section to play with me. She would climb on my lap and cry. I felt like I was her mom. She was only four."

"Did you wonder where Valeria was?" I ask.

"I was too little to know she wasn't with us."

Morgan assumed Valeria was with them somewhere in the orphanage, but she didn't know where. She didn't know why all this was happening. She can only say it was all so confusing.

A little backstory on Russian orphanages. Children are separated by age and divided into living quarters to suit their size and development. Babies, toddlers, and kids up to age five typically live in baby homes that are equipped with cribs and toddler beds. Kids five and up are transferred to an orphanage, where they live and go to school until they age out at eighteen, unless parents come back or they are adopted. Both are very rare.

"I can see how you wouldn't know where she was," I remark.

Morgan says she never saw Valeria after the shelter. Weeks turned into months. She fell into a daily routine, walking with the other kids to school in the village, practicing math equations, learning Cyrillic, and playing outside on the playground like normal kids do. But it was far from normal without her mom. Thankfully, she saw Katya every day after school. Katya was her comfort, and Morgan was hers.

A year and some months later, still without mom, the unexpected happened: the girls were given an opportunity to be adopted.

"I didn't know what that meant. I was sad I didn't have my mom," she says, "but I don't remember feeling sad about being adopted."

That summer the two sisters, now five and eight, along with a busload of other kids from the same orphanage, were flown to the US through arrangements made by an adoption agency in Maryland.

"We went on an airplane for the first time," she says. "I mostly slept. We didn't know what was happening. We rode a bus to a building or church or something to meet our host family. Katya and I were crying and scared. We were hungry and tired."

After arriving at her host family's townhouse, she describes how the people—she didn't know what to call them—gave them fruit, comforted them, and tucked them into bed together in their own room.

"Katya and I huddled together that night," she says. They wondered where they were and what was going on and who these people were. They clung to each other all night, finally falling into a restless sleep.

The next morning, she says, they were too afraid to go downstairs and talk to "the people." She remembers a woman came to the house who could speak Russian to them. It helped them feel better, sort of.

The next five weeks were a lot like camp, she says.

"We learned how to swim in a pool. We played with our new cousins. We put our feet in warm sand at the beach. We tasted new foods. I found out I was picky."

"Seriously," I laugh. "Picky?"

Then I thought about it. Kids in orphanages eat what's served. Beach corn dogs, poolside snacks, and pasta with cousins were all yummy new experiences. Having choices was too. It was all so new.

The five weeks flew by. The girls returned to the orphanage. Meanwhile, official documents were prepared so they could be adopted.

"We were officially adopted a few months later in December. I was thrilled that Katya and I were able to stay together," she admits. She was receiving the good that God was giving her. She was seeing the possibilities of her new life as best she could.

For the second time, the girls were escorted from Russia to the US.

Alongside their new family, the sisters went to school, tripped over English, made friends, received American Girl Doll look-alikes, had sleepovers, and adjusted to their new life as best they could. Over the years, Morgan felt her loss. It was painful. She pushed it away, met with counselors, accepted what had happened to her, eventually refocused on what she has that is good, and ultimately found out that being thankful changes how she feels. It was a process that didn't happen overnight.

Two years after the girls were adopted, their mom got a call that their sister Valeria had been adopted too, by a couple in Michigan . . . my husband and me.

"You were a preteen. What was going through your mind?" I ask.

"I was giddy because I had only seen her when she was first born," Morgan says. The girls were now five, eight, and almost twelve.

Thankful and thrilled would not begin to describe how she felt to see her sister again for the first time in several years.

"She was so cute. She wasn't a baby anymore. She was talking. She was so much younger than me," she adds. "It was great getting to know another person who was biologically related to me. Knowing that there is another part of me in the States makes me feel much more connected.

"When we are with Valeria, we can tell she is our sister. I can tell she is the same as us. Sometimes she acts like Katya and sometimes she acts like me. She has a mix. Katya and I act totally different. Our personalities, and the way we handle situations, are different. She's more extroverted. I am more introverted. Valeria is a mix of both of us.

"We try to see each other once a year. I love that Valeria gets to be a part of my life even if she doesn't live with me. I love watching her grow up. I am very thankful that we got the opportunity to have this amazing sisterly relationship forever."

Over the past fourteen years Morgan has experienced resilience in the wake of emotional trauma. Losing her biological mother, her home, her sister, her country, her language as a child—these are losses she shouldn't have experienced. She was abandoned, frightened, and wounded emotionally. While her sorrow has subsided, and she is opening up more and more about the past, she also realizes that her reality is much better when she is thankful. She is thankful for second chances. She is thankful her spirit is intact. She is thankful for her family. In her own way, Morgan is choosing to be thankful not as a way to deny her feelings, but because it is the gateway to resetting her heart.

CONCLUSION

MOVING FORWARD

Kindred spirits are not so scarce as I used to think. It's splendid to find out there are so many of them in the world.

L. M. MONTGOMERY

WHEN I WAS gathering true stories from young adult adoptees around the nation, I looked for voices that would resonate with you. I searched for kindred spirits a few steps ahead who could tell it like it is but also offer advice, encouragement, inspiration, and hope. You've heard from high schoolers, athletes, college students, grad students, and people in professions of all kinds. They are happy, funny, honest, caring, amazing people who are processing their feelings and actively participating in their own getting well. Can you believe you've had a front-row seat, the first of its kind? I hope you find yourself saying, "Finally, someone gets me," and "I'm not the only one."

What's next?

It's up to you. This book is not a fix, more like an invitation to consider whether you have work to do too. Opening up is uncomfortable, even for my kids. At eighteen, my daughter made her first attempt at opening up when she handed me a four-by-eight-inch manila envelope, the kind with the circle and metal clasp that keeps things sealed tight inside. I looked at her, held the envelope in my hand, turned it over, looking for something, a sign that would identify what was inside. Something felt ominous. On the very bottom right-hand corner, in tiny print, a date and her name.

"What's this?" I raised my eyebrows, curious. She motioned for me to look inside.

I opened the clasp and slipped out a crudely cut, two-by-two-inch small chunk of cardboard. The words "Not good enough" were written across it, whispering from its hiding place as if no one should know. I looked in her eyes, at her beautiful face, her hair in a messy bun, and took a deep breath. She had summed up her self-worth in three words. No wonder the last few years had been a mix of unexpected ups and downs. Her false belief held her heart and mind captive and made her into something she is not. I checked the date again and did the math. She had written it four years earlier at church camp.

"Mom, what people see daily is silly, crazy, sometimes mellow me. But inside I have more mind battles than most," she confessed, heading into the kitchen.

"Why didn't you tell me?" I asked.

"I don't let a lot of people in on my deep thoughts. It's just easier."

She was making an attempt to open up. I was thrilled and scared for both of us. The only thing I could draw on to make sense of this, other than normal teen angst, was her separation story and how it impacts her. She has a double separation story, separated first from her birth mother, then separated a second time from her caregivers, whom she was attached to, at the baby home. How scary. She was one and a half years old when we adopted her. All this happened before she could talk or process or grieve what she lost. Deep down, she carries the irrational fear that she isn't good enough. At the root of it all is fear, a fear that she can't put into words.

What's going on?

I turned to my friend Kurt Ellis, a seasoned adoption therapist (and the guy who read all the stories in this book).[1] He says, "It is impossible not to have residual feelings and questions from such a significant event."

My mind clings to the word *residual*. It sounds sticky, like something has stuck after all these years. That explains it!

Kurt continues, "Anyone reading this needs to know there is not something wrong with them, but that something happened to them!"

But Kurt doesn't end there.

"The only way to break the influence of the past is to work through it," he says.

"That's what I like about this book. It is honest. It gives everyone hope that they can make it through, because others have made it through and have learned to thrive. It shows that there is a process, and while it can be hard for some, especially for those who struggle, it's doable."

Kurt emphasizes, "I think readers will see themselves in a story and say, 'That's me!' And believe it will be all right. Some may think they are always going to feel this way. But it's not true. They also think they are the only ones. They are not."

You may have noticed one quirky detail about this book: that the gritty details are missing. It's true. Each story is like watching a half-hour TV show, where a problem is easily resolved in thirty minutes. Obviously, each story has been a process with different approaches. There is not enough time to dig into all the details or all the work they did. Though it may appear this was an easy journey for some, in truth it was a long and difficult road.

My heart soars to have Kurt lend us some help to conclude this collection of stories.

I hope after reading these stories that you've come away better equipped to process what you hold in your heart. The storytellers, the siblinghood, realize that their growth wasn't just for them. It was also for you to learn from. Just like your growth is for others too. If you'd like to stay in touch visit me at susantebos.com. I pray these stories have unlocked new ways of thinking and responding to life's ups and downs, and will help you become more of who God created you to be.

ACKNOWLEDGMENTS

MY HUMBLE THANKS . . .

To all the storytellers who shared their lives with me over grande-size chai, mochas, lunch, FaceTime, phone calls, and on front porches. Know that my thanks is not enough.

To a certain group of moms who sat around that table for weeks trying to makes sense of relinquishment and its effects on our kids. The birth of this book started there, with you.

To my family and friends who have supported me, listened for countless hours, and believed in me and this project. Your encouragement and prayers have carried me.

To Cynthia Beach, Jamie Brummel, Savanna Clark, Margot Starbuck, Lera TeBos, and so many others for being there every step of the way.

To Kurt Ellis and Families Forever Counseling, and Kathryn Lewis-Ginebaugh, PsyD, clinical psychologist, for reviewing these pages prior to publication.

To the hardworking team at Kregel Publications, for investing mega hours and expertise, and for seeing the benefit of this book.

To my husband, Mike, your constant support over the years means everything to me. You had me at tomato.

To our children, Matthew, Kola, and Lera. I am forever thankful to be your mom.

THE SOMEWHERE IN BETWEEN CLUB

I WANDERED MY way through the MSU Union at Michigan State University, past the iconic, buff bronze statue of Sparty lounging on a park bench in his Roman wear, face as fierce as the teams he represents, making my way to meet the Somewhere In Between Club. The club is a hub for students who are adopted and want to find a place to connect, eat food, and share life. I asked the club if they would be willing to share some advice with you. They jumped on the chance. In fact, they sent out a request to club alumni too.

So, from them to you:

- Your feelings are not wrong. If you feel sad or angry, it's okay. It is normal.
- Don't feel forced to fit into a category of a "race."
- No matter how alone you feel, just know that other adoptees have shared the same experiences.
- Blood doesn't make you a family.
- If you are interested in learning about your culture, don't be afraid to go outside your comfort zone and learn something new. But don't feel like you have to.

- Try to reach out to other adoptees to share experiences and stories.
- Everyone has their own journey to finding themselves.
- A lot of adoptees are perfectionists. It's okay. Identity is more complex than it seems.
- Some of you are going to experience racism from all races.
- Don't feel bad if you don't know your culture or speak the language.
- Don't be afraid to tell your family about how you're feeling.
- People will say ignorant things, but don't let that affect you. Use ignorance as an opportunity to educate.
- It's okay to be curious about finding your birth family.
- Have fun taking a DNA test! Some tests will give you character traits that will tell you if you have the genes for a specific trait (such as disliking cilantro, or having flat feet or long toes, or being prone to mosquito bites).
- Be patient with your DNA results. It could be months or years after you take a DNA test that you find someone who matches you. Also, know that there's a high chance you never find your birth family. You aren't alone.

XXOO Somewhere In Between Club, Michigan State University

NOTES

Section 1—Dare to Overcome: Wrestling Is a Part of Life

1. Kelli Worrall and Peter Worrall, *20 Things We'd Tell Our Twenty-something Selves* (Chicago: Moody, 2015), 59.

2. Sarah Weinberg, "Baking Is the Best Way to Alleviate Stress—Yes, Really," *Delish*, March 25, 2020, https://www.delish.com/food/a31669795/stress-baking/.

Section 3—Trust Again: It's Worth the Risk

1. Health Insurance Portability and Accountability Act.

Section 4—Search for Answers . . . or Not: It's Normal, Okay, and Expected

1. For more information about China's One Child Policy, see Matt Soniak, "How Does China Enforce Its One-Baby Policy?" *Mental Floss*, January 5, 2012, https://www.mentalfloss.com/article/29647/how-does-china-enforce-its-one-baby-policy.

2. You can learn more about the largest family in the world, Mully Children's Family, at https://www.mullychildrensfamily.org/about/.

Section 5—Acceptance: A Natural Remedy for Peace

1. Nancy Verrier's *The Primal Wound: Understanding the Adopted Child* is a great resource for any parents looking for additional insight.

Conclusion—Moving Forward

1. Kurt Ellis is a therapist at Families Forever Counseling in Grand Rapids, Michigan. Find out more about him and his practice at www.familiesforevercounseling.com.

Epigraphs

Section 1—Dare to Overcome: Wrestling Is a Part of Life

Chapter 1: *Harry Potter and the Half-Blood Prince*

Notes

Chapter 2: *Harry Potter and the Order of the Phoenix*

Chapter 3: *Christopher Robin* (2018)

Chapter 5: *Salt from My Attic*

Chapter 8: *The Body Keeps the Score: Brain, Mind, and Body in the Healing of Trauma*

Section 2—You're Not Alone: We've Been There Too

Section Page: *The World According to Mister Rogers: Important Things to Remember*

Chapter 9: https://www.imdb.com/name/nm0034314/

Chapter 10: *The Vital Balance: The Life Process in Mental Health and Illness*

Chapter 11: https://healingbrave.com/blogs/all/quotes-about-healing-from -trauma

Section 3—Trust Again: It's Worth the Risk

Section Page: *You Are Special: Neighborly Words from Mister Rogers*

Chapter 14: *Do Hard Things: A Teenage Rebellion Against Low Expectations*

Chapter 17: *A Long Way Home*

Chapter 18: https://www.misterrogers.org/

Section 4—Search for Answers . . . or Not: It's Normal, Okay, and Expected

Chapter 20: *Great Expectations*

Chapter 23: www.searchquotes.com

Chapter 24: *A Long Way Home*

Chapter 25: *Free Solo* (2018)

Section 5—Acceptance: A Natural Remedy for Peace

Chapter 26: https://www.sideeffectspublicmedia.org/community-health/2015 -02-03/childhood-trauma-leads-to-brains-wired-for-fear

Chapter 27: quotefancy.com

Chapter 29: *Harry Potter and the Order of the Phoenix*

Chapter 30: *The World According to Mister Rogers: Important Things to Remember*

Chapter 31: www.searchquotes.com

Chapter 33: *One Thousand Gifts: A Dare to Live Fully Right Where You Are*

Conclusion—Moving Forward: *Anne of Green Gables*